Hidden Treasures
In the Biblical Text

By
Chuck Missler

Koinonia House

Hidden Treasures

Copyright 2000 by Chuck Missler

Published by Koinonia House
P.O. Box D
Coeur d'Alene ID 83816-0347
 www.khouse.org

First printing, December, 2000
Seventh printing, March, 2006

ISBN: 978-1-57821-127-2

All Scripture quotations are from the King James Version of the Holy Bible.

PRINTED IN THE UNITED STATES OF AMERICA

Table of Contents

This book contains many highlights from *Cosmic Codes - Hidden Messages From the Edge of Eternity,* also published by Koinonia House.

Warning:

This book can prove seriously disruptive to the comfort of closely held presuppositions.

This little book may well change your entire perspective on the Bible and it may alter your own most cherished priorities.

It may seem old-fashioned to take the Bible seriously, especially in our modern age of scientific discoveries and multicultural emphases. It has become politically correct to deny the existence of absolutes and to deny the involvement of our Creator in our affairs. And yet there are many intellectual and well-informed people who take the Bible *very* seriously—who even regard its origin as supernatural. Why?

My own personal background has been in the information sciences—computers, communication, cryptography, and the like. With graduate degrees in engineering and business, and having spent a 30-year career in the corporate boardrooms of over a dozen high-tech enterprises, I have become most profoundly impressed by two astonishing discoveries:

1) The 66 books which we call the Bible constitute a highly integrated message system. What makes this so astonishing is the fact that they were penned by more than forty different people over a period of several thousand years![1] Yet we now discover that virtually every detail of the

Biblical text evidences a highly skillful *integrated* design from cover to cover. In fact, every word, every place name, every detail was apparently placed there (in the original) deliberately as part of an overall intricate plan.

2) What is even more astounding is that it can be *demonstrated* that the origin of this intricate design is from outside of our dimension of space and time.

The Nature of Time

While philosophers throughout history have debated almost every idea under the sun since the world began, the one thing that they all have presumed–from the beginning–is that time is *linear* and *absolute*. Most of us assume that a minute a thousand years ago is the same as a minute today, and that we live in a dimension in which time inexorably rolls onward, yet is totally intractable to any attempt to glimpse ahead. Traversing the dimension of time remains the ever popular realm of fiction writers, and, apparently, a few strange experiments of the particle physicists.[2]

This linear view of time is exemplified by our frequent use of "time lines." When we were in school, our teachers would draw a line on the blackboard. The left end of the line might represent the beginning of something–the birth of a person, or the founding of a nation, or the start of an era. The right end of the line would demark the termination of that subject–the death of a person or the ending of an era.

Begin _____ End

(Now?)

Therefore, when we consider the concept of "eternity," we tend to view it as a *line of infinite length*–from "infinity" on the left and continuing toward "infinity" on the right.

$-\infty$　　　　　　　　　　　　　　　　　　　$+\infty$

When we think of "God," we naturally assume that He is someone "with lots of time."

But this linear view suffers from the misconceptions carried over from an obsolete physics. Today we owe a great debt to the efforts of Dr. Albert Einstein.

It was the insight of Dr. Einstein, in considering the nature of our physical universe, that we live in more than just three dimensions, and that time itself is a *fourth* physical dimension. This insight led to his famous General Theory of Relativity–and to the discovery that time itself is also part of our *physical* reality.

> *People like us, who believe in physics, know that the distinction between past, present, and the future is only a stubbornly persistent illusion.*
>
> – Albert Einstein

The Dimensions of Reality

We now realize that we live in (at least) four dimensions: not just the three spatial dimensions of length, width and height, but also with an additional *physical* dimension of time.[3] Time is now known to be a *physical* property–and that time *varies* with mass, acceleration and gravity.

A time measurement device in a weaker gravitational field runs faster than one in a stronger field. Near the surface of the Earth the frequency of an atomic clock decreases about one part in 10^{16} per meter, and, thus, a clock 100 meters higher than a reference clock will have a frequency greater by one part in 10^{14}.

Most discussions of the physics of time will also include the interesting case of two hypothetical astronauts born at the same instant. One remains on the Earth; the other is sent on a space mission to the nearest star, Alpha Centauri, about 4 ½ light years distant. If his vehicle travels at a speed of half the velocity of light, when our traveler returns to the Earth he would be more than *two years younger* than his twin brother![4] (If that doesn't bother you, you weren't paying attention!)

Our Common Misconception

Is God subject to gravity? Is *He* subject to the constraints of mass or acceleration? Hardly.

God is not someone "who has lots of time": He is *outside* the domain of time altogether. That is what Isaiah means when he says, "It is He who *inhabits eternity.*"[5]

Since God has the technology to create us in the first place, He certainly has the technology to get a message to us. But how does He *authenticate* His message? How does He assure us that the message is really from Him and not a fraud or a contrivance?

One way to authenticate the message is to demonstrate that its source is from *outside* of our time domain. God declares, "I alone know the end from the beginning."[6] His message includes history written in advance.

An illustrative example is that of a parade. As we might sit on the curb and observe the many bands, marching units, floats, and other elements coming around the corner and passing in front of us, the parade is–to us–clearly a *sequence* of events. However, to someone who is *outside the plane of the parade's existence*–say, in a helicopter above the city–the beginning and the end can be *simultaneously* in view.

(It is amazing how many theological paradoxes evaporate when one recognizes the restrictions of viewing our predicament solely from within our own time dimension.)[7]

A Message of Extraterrestrial Origin

Many have said, "You can't 'prove' the Bible." Withhold your own judgment on this issue until you have finished this book. Some of the implications of these "hidden treasures" may surprise you.

We are in possession of this collection of 66 books we call The Bible, written by more than 40 authors over several thousands of years, yet we now discover it is an *integrated* message from *outside* our time domain. It repeatedly authenticates this uniqueness by describing history *before* it happens. And this discovery totally shatters our traditional concepts of reality.

This little book, gleaned from a lifetime of collecting, highlights only a few of the remarkable discoveries that reveal the astonishing realities lying behind the Biblical text, which we trust will elevate your appreciation for the uniqueness of its message and its implications for you personally.

We hope you find it disruptive to the comfort of your presuppositions; disturbing, provocative, yet desperately helpful.

Selection One

Hidden in Plain Sight

*It is the glory of God to conceal a thing:
but the honour of kings is to search out a matter.*

Proverbs 25:2

Are there hidden messages in the Bible? Some say no. Let us look further.

It comes as a surprise to many that there *are* numerous hidden messages in the Bible, and one of the most remarkable is hidden in a genealogy in Genesis Chapter 5.[8] This is one of those Chapters which we often tend to skim over quickly as we pass through Genesis; after all, it's only a genealogy of ten people, from Adam to Noah.

But God always rewards the diligent student. Let's examine this Chapter more closely.

In our Bible, we read the ten *Hebrew* names: Adam, Seth, Enosh, Kenan, Mahalalel, Jared, Enoch, Methuselah, Lamech, and Noah. Since these are proper names, they are not translated, but only *transliterated* to approximate the way they were pronounced. But what do these names *signify* in English?

Original Roots Needed

The meaning of proper names can be a difficult pursuit since a direct translation is usually not readily available. Even a conventional Hebrew lexicon can prove disappointing. Many study aids, such as a conventional lexicon, can prove superficial when dealing with proper names. A study of the original *roots*, however, can yield some fascinating insights. (However, views concerning the meaning of original roots are not free of controversy and variant readings.)

The Mystery of Methuselah

Here is a question to ask your Biblically literate friends: if Methuselah was the oldest man in the Bible, how could he die *before* his father? That's a real puzzler to most people!

That's because most people forget who Methuselah's father was: His father was Enoch, who didn't die, but was caught up directly to heaven.[9] Enoch also happens to be one of the most fascinating characters in the Old Testament.

The Flood of Noah did not come as a surprise. It had been preached on for four generations. But something strange happened when Enoch was 65, from which time "he walked with God." Enoch was given a prophecy of the coming Great Flood, and was apparently told that as long as his son was alive, the judgment of the Flood would be withheld; but as soon as he died, the Flood would be sent forth.

Enoch named his son to reflect this prophecy. The name Methuselah comes from two roots: מות, *muth*, a root that means "death"[10]; and from שלח, *shalach*, which means "to bring," or "to send forth." Thus, the name Methuselah signifies, "his death shall bring."[11]

(Can you imagine raising that kid? Every time the boy caught a cold, the entire neighborhood must have panicked!)

And, indeed, in the year that Methuselah died, the flood came. Methuselah was 187 when he had Lamech, and lived 782 years more. Lamech had Noah when he was 182.[12] The Flood came in Noah's 600th year.[13] 187 + 182 + 600 = 969, the year Methuselah died.[14]

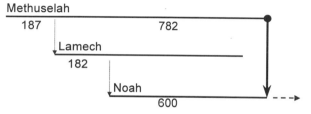

It is interesting that Methuselah's life was, in effect, a symbol of God's mercy in forestalling the coming judgment of the Flood. It is therefore fitting that his lifetime is the oldest in the Bible, symbolizing the extreme extensiveness of God's mercy.

The Other Names

Since there is such significance in Methuselah's name, let's examine the other names to discover what may lie behind them. (Bear with me on this: it'll be worth it!)

The first name, Adam, אָדָם, *adomah*, means "man." As the first man, that seems straightforward enough.

Adam's son was named Seth, שֵׁת, which means "appointed." When he was born Eve said, "For God hath *appointed* me another seed instead of Abel, whom Cain slew."[15]

Seth's son was called Enosh, אֱנוֹשׁ, which means "mortal," "frail," or "miserable." It is from the root *anash*: to be incurable, used of a wound, grief, woe, sickness, or wickedness.

It was in the days of Enosh that men began to defile the name of the Living God.[16]

Enosh's son was named Kenan, from קֵינָן which can mean "sorrow," dirge," or "elegy." (The precise denotation is somewhat elusive; some study aids unfortunately presume that Kenan is synonymous with "Cainan." Balaam, looking down from the heights of Moab, employed a pun upon the name of the Kenites when he prophesied their destruction.[17])

We have no real idea as to why these names were chosen for their children. Often they may have referred to circumstances at their birth, etc.

Kenan's son was Mahalalel, from מַהֲלַל, which means "blessed" or "praise"; and אֵל *El*, the name for God. Thus, Mahalalel means "the Blessed God." Often Hebrew names included *El*, the name of God, as Dani-*el*, "God is my Judge," Nathani-*el*, "Gift of God," etc.

Mahalalel's son was named Jared, יֶרֶד, from the verb *yaradh*, meaning "shall come down." Some authorities suggest that this might be an allusion to the "Sons of God" who "came down" to corrupt the daughters of men, resulting in the *Nephilim* ("fallen ones") of Genesis 6. [18]

Jared's son was named Enoch, חֲנוֹךְ, which means "teaching," or "commencement." He was the first of four generations of preachers. In fact, the earliest recorded prophecy was by Enoch, which, amazingly enough, deals with the Second Coming of Christ (although it is quoted in the Book of Jude in the New Testament):

> *And Enoch also, the seventh from Adam, prophesied of these, saying, Behold, the Lord cometh with ten thousands of his saints,*
> *To execute judgement upon all, and to convince all that are ungodly among them of all their ungodly deeds which they have ungodly committed, and of all their hard speeches which ungodly sinners have spoken against him.*
> Jude 14,15

Enoch was the father of Methuselah, whom we have already mentioned. Enoch walked with God *after* he begat Methuselah.[19] Apparently, Enoch received the prophecy of the Great Flood, and was told that as long as his son was alive, the judgment of the Flood would be withheld. The year that Methuselah died, the Flood came.

Methuselah's son was named Lamech, לֶמֶךְ, a root still evident today in our own English word, "lament" or "lamentation." Lamech suggests "despairing."

(This name is also linked to the Lamech in Cain's line who inadvertently killed his son Tubal-Cain in a hunting incident.[20])

Lamech, of course, is the father of Noah, נח, which is derived from *nacham*, "to bring relief" or "comfort," as Lamech himself explains:

> *And he called his name Noah, saying, This*
> *same shall **comfort** us concerning our work and*
> *toil of our hands, because of the ground which*
> *the LORD hath cursed.*   Genesis 5:29

The Composite List

Now let's put it all together:

Hebrew	*English*
Adam	Man
Seth	Appointed
Enosh	Mortal
Kenan	Sorrow;
Mahalalel	The Blessed God
Jared	Shall come down
Enoch	Teaching
Methuselah	His death shall bring
Lamech	The despairing
Noah	Rest, or comfort

That's remarkable:

"Man (is) appointed mortal sorrow; (but) the Blessed
God shall come down teaching (that) His death shall
bring (the) despairing rest."

Here is a summary of God's plan of redemption, hidden here within a genealogy in Genesis! You will never convince me that a group of Jewish rabbis deliberately contrived to hide a summary of the Christian Gospel right here in a genealogy within their venerated Torah!

Evidences of Design

The implications of this discovery are far more deeply significant than may be evident at first glance. It demonstrates that in the earliest Chapters of the Book of Genesis, God had already laid out His plan of redemption for the predicament of mankind. It is the beginning of a love story, ultimately written in blood on a wooden cross which was erected in Judea almost 2,000 years ago.

This is also one of many evidences that the Bible is an *integrated* message system, the product of supernatural engineering. This punctures the presumptions of many who view the Bible as a record of an evolving cultural tradition, noble though it may be. It claims to be authored by the One who alone knows the end from the beginning.[21]

It is astonishing to discover how many Biblical "controversies" seem to evaporate if one simply recognizes the unity–the *integrity*–of these 66 books. Every number, every place name, every detail–every *jot* and tittle–is part of a tightly engineered design, tailored for our learning, our discovery, and our amazement.

Bibliography:

Missler, Chuck, *Cosmic Codes - Hidden Messages From the Edge of Eternity*, Koinonia House, 1999.

Jones, Alfred, *Dictionary of Old Testament Proper Names*, Kregel Publications, Grand Rapids, MI, 1990.

Kaplan, Rabbi Aryeh, *The Living Torah*, Maznaim Publishing Corporation, Jerusalem, 1981.

Pink, Arthur W., *Gleanings in Genesis*, Moody Bible Institute, Chicago IL, 1922.

Rosenbaum, M., and Silbermann, A., *Pentateuch with Onkelos's Translation (into Aramaic) and Rashi's Commentary*, Silbermann Family Publishers, Jerusalem, 1973.

Stedman, Ray C., *The Beginnings*, Word Books, Waco, TX, 1978.

Selection Two

The Skipping of Letters

The secrets of the Torah are revealed...
in the skipping of the letters.

Rabbi Moses Cordevaro, 16th century

Mention the term "Bible Code" to almost anyone, and they immediately think of a particular type of code called the "Equidistant Letter Sequence," or ELS, popularized by a number of recent books and considered quite controversial by most observers. There are, however, some unique aspects of the Biblical text that are hard to ignore.

Weissmandl

The recent flurry of interest in "Equidistant Letter Sequences" in the Bible is due, in large measure, to the discoveries of Rabbi Michael Ber Weissmandl, who, at the age of 13, acquired a Torah commentary written by a 13th century sage, Rabbenu Bachya ben Asher of Saragossa, in Spain. Fascinated by Bachya's cryptic asides, and allusions to decryptions, Weissmandl maintained his certainty that divinely ordered information was embedded in the Torah by means of Bachya's description of the *skipping of equal intervals of letters.*[22] Even as a youth Weissmandl wrote out the entire 304,805 letters of the Torah in 10 by 10 grids (a common practice in cryptanalysis to facilitate the identification of skipped-letter sequences).

Weissmandl's pursuit of these mysteries ostensibly hidden
in the Torah was interrupted by the arrival of the Nazis, his
escape from the train taking him and his family to Auschwitz,
and his subsequent exploits in organizing Schindler-like
ransom efforts to extricate Jews from their tragic fates.[23]

Weissmandl's Strange Legacy

(The following was first revealed to me by my friend, Dr.
Gerald Schroeder, the famed atomic physicist who presently
resides in Jerusalem.[24])

Here are the opening verses in the Book of Genesis in
Hebrew: (Remember, Hebrew goes from right to left!)

בְּרֵאשִׁת בָּרָא אֱלֹהִים אֵת הַשָּׁמַיִם וְאֵת הָאָרֶץ:
וְהָאָרֶץ הָיְתָה תֹהוּ וָבֹהוּ וְחֹשֶׁךְ עַל־פְּנֵי תְהוֹם וְרוּחַ
אֱלֹהִים מְרַחֶפֶת עַל־פְּנֵי הַמָּיִם:
וַיֹּאמֶר אֱלֹהִים יְהִי אוֹר וַיְהִי־אוֹר:
וַיַּרְא אֱלֹהִים אֶת־הָאוֹר כִּי־טוֹב וַיַּבְדֵּל אֱלֹהִים בֵּין הָאוֹר
וּבֵין הַחֹשֶׁךְ:
וַיִּקְרָא אֱלֹהִים לָאוֹר יוֹם וְלַחֹשֶׁךְ קָרָא לָיְלָה וַיְהִי־עֶרֶב
וַיְהִי־בֹקֶר יוֹם אֶחָד: פ

The word *Torah*, in Hebrew, is four letters, תּוֹרָה. If you go
to the first ת (*tau*, which is similar to our "T"), and count an
interval of 49 letters, the next letter is a ו (*vav*, operating here
like an "O"); count another interval of 49 letters and you will
find a ר (*resh*, like our "R"); and then count another interval
of 49 letters and you will find a ה (*heh*, or "H"). We find

the word תורה, or Torah, spelled out at 49 letter intervals. Rather strange. It would seem that someone has gone to some remarkable effort; and yet some argue that it is just coincidence.

And when we examine the next book, the Book of Exodus, we discover the same thing again! Here are the first few verses of Exodus:

וְאֵלֶּה שְׁמוֹת בְּנֵי יִשְׂרָאֵל הַבָּאִים מִצְרָיְמָה אֵת יַעֲקֹב אִישׁ וּבֵיתוֹ בָּאוּ:
רְאוּבֵן שִׁמְעוֹן לֵוִי וִיהוּדָה:
יִשָּׂשכָר זְבוּלֻן וּבְנְיָמִן:
דָּן וְנַפְתָּלִי גָּד וְאָשֵׁר:
וַיְהִי כָּל־נֶפֶשׁ יֹצְאֵי יֶרֶךְ־יַעֲקֹב שִׁבְעִים נָפֶשׁ וְיוֹסֵף הָיָה בְמִצְרָיִם:
וַיָּמָת יוֹסֵף וְכָל־אֶחָיו וְכֹל הַדּוֹר הַהוּא:

Could this also be a coincidence, *again*? Just what are the chances of such a coincidence? The word תורה might, on merely a statistical basis, appear in Genesis quite a few times depending on the range of intervals chosen. The total number of letters in Genesis is 78,064, and the number of the letter ת, 4152; ו, 8448; ר, 4793, and ה, 6283. Indeed, תורה appears three times in Genesis at the interval of 50, which is what might be statistically expected from a book of that length and of similar concentration of these four letters. But there is no reason why these should begin with the *first* ת of the book, and why this should happen in *both* Genesis and Exodus. The probability of such a coincidence has been estimated at about one in three million!

In the next book, the Book of Leviticus, this 49-letter interval doesn't seem to appear. (We'll return to reexamine an alternative discovery.)

When we examine the next book, the Book of Numbers,
we discover that it happens again *if* we spell Torah
backwards!

וַיְדַבֵּר יְהוָה אֶל־מֹשֶׁה בְּמִדְבַּר סִינַי בְּאֹהֶל מוֹעֵד בְּאֶחָד
לַחֹדֶשׁ הַשֵּׁנִי בַּשָּׁנָה הַשֵּׁנִית לְצֵאתָם מֵאֶרֶץ מִצְרַיִם לֵאמֹר:
שְׂאוּ אֶת־רֹאשׁ כָּל־עֲדַת בְּנֵי־יִשְׂרָאֵל לְמִשְׁפְּחֹתָם לְבֵית
אֲבֹתָם בְּמִסְפַּר שֵׁמוֹת כָּל־זָכָר לְגֻלְגְּלֹתָם:
מִבֶּן עֶשְׂרִים שָׁנָה וָמַעְלָה כָּל־יֹצֵא צָבָא בְּיִשְׂרָאֵל תִּפְקְדוּ
אֹתָם לְצִבְאֹתָם אַתָּה וְאַהֲרֹן:

When we examine the final book of the Torah, the Book of
Deuteronomy, a similar thing happens,[25] but again,
backwards! Laying out the overall pattern:

Genesis	Exodus	Leviticus	Numbers	Deuteronomy
TORH ⟶	TORH ⟶	?	⟵ HROT	⟵ HROT

This seems to be too deliberate to be ascribed simply to
chance. But why has this ostensibly deliberate arrangement
been composed? What are the implications?

When we return to reexamine the Book of Leviticus, we
discover that the *square root* of 49, 7, yields a provocative
result. After the first *yod* (י), and an interval of seven, taking
the next letter yields הוהי, the tetragramaton, the ineffable
name of God, the YHWH. It appears that the *Torah always
points toward the Ineffable Name of God!*

Genesis	Exodus	Leviticus	Numbers	Deuteronomy
TORH ⟶	TORH ⟶	YHWH	⟵ HROT	⟵ HROT

This seems to hint of a hidden signature. Just as certain
authors adopted a trademark, or "shtick," such as Alfred

Hitchcock always appearing as an extra in his famous movies, or J.M.W. Turner's secret signature on his venerated water colors, or the fabled hidden signature of Shakespeare in Psalm 46,[26] we detect here evidence of hidden but *deliberate* design. And it may be a signpost pointing to others.

As we discovered in the previous Chapter, within the first of the five books of Moses, known in Hebrew as the Torah, God's redemptive program was anticipated in the hidden message in the genealogy of Noah. Even the very name of this most venerated part of the Old Testament highlights God's program.

Even the word "Torah" itself, drawing on the concepts that lie behind the original Hebrew letters, תורה, embodies some provocative elements: The *Tav* (originally, a cross), the *Vav* (a nail), the *Resh* (the head of a *man*), and the *Heh*, (the breath or Spirit of God). Thus, Man, with the Spirit of God, nailed on the Cross! This term was in existence well before Messiah walked on the earth.

It is an interesting summary of the climax of God's love story, which was nailed on a cross erected in Judea 2,000 years ago. The entire Biblical drama records the extremes our Creator has resorted to in order to redeem man–including you and me–from our predicament.

Could this *hidden design* be simply an accident? There are those that argue that this is all a result of random chance. There are others who simply ascribe this remarkable structure to some ancient "diddling" by a clever scribe. However, we will discover that this all appears to be part of an even larger design. This discovery by Weissmandl appears to be only a *remez*, a hint of something hidden or something deeper.

It would be Weissmandl's rediscoveries of the ancient sages that subsequently inspired the Israeli researchers, 60 years later and armed with computers, to uncover what has now erupted into the modern day controversies, codes which appear to describe events which transcend the time period in which they were written: the events surrounding the revolt of the Maccabees; the storming of the Bastille during the French revolution; the Holocaust in Germany; the treatment of diabetes; a description of AIDS; and many specifics of current history. However, it is beyond the scope of this brief review to explore the validity of some of the more fanciful claims regarding these codes and to adequately review the serious caveats regarding their implications.[27] (We will look at one of the most provocative of these in Chapter 9.)

* * *

Bibliography

Missler, Chuck, *Cosmic Codes - Hidden Messages From the Edge of Eternity*, Koinonia House, 1999.

Jeffrey Satinover, *Cracking the Bible Code*, William Morrow and Co., New York 1997.

Gerald L. Schroeder, *Genesis and the Big Bang,* Bantam Books, New York, 1990.

Selection Three

The Rule of Seven

God does not play dice.
–Albert Einstein
(If He did, He'd win.)

The recurrence of seven–or an exact multiple of seven–is found throughout the Bible and is widely recognized. The frequent occurrence of the number seven is conspicuous even to a casual reader.

We encounter the seven days of Creation in Genesis, the seven Feasts of Israel, seven days of rain after Noah enters the ark, seven days between the doves, Jacob serves seven years for each of his two wives, seven kine and ears of corn in Pharaoh's dreams (seven good years and seven famine years), seven lamps of the Menorah, the seven elements of furniture in the Tabernacle, seven days of the feast of unleavened bread, the repeated use of seven in the Levitical priestly instructions, the seven weeks to the Feast of Weeks, the seven months between Nisan and Tishri, (and the seven years of the sabbatical year, and the seven times seven to the Jubilee Year); the seven priests with seven trumpets circling Jericho seven times in the Book of Joshua, seven nations of Canaan, Solomon was seven years building the Temple, Naaman washed seven times in the river, seven loaves fed the four thousand, etc.

In the Book of Revelation we encounter seven churches, seven lampstands, seven stars, seven seals, seven horns, seven spirits of God, seven angels, seven trumpets, seven thunders, seven crowns, seven last plagues, seven bowls, seven kings, and there are many more sevens, much more subtle in their presence.

The more one examines the text more closely, the more evident is the recurrence of seven, and sometimes in some very surprising ways.

A Design Challenge

Consider the following assignment: Try designing a genealogy–even from fiction–which meets the following criteria:

1) The number of **words** in it must be divisible by 7 *evenly*. (In each of these constraints, it is assumed that the resulting divisions are without any remainders.)

2) The number of **letters** must also be divisible by 7.

   (Not too difficult so far? Let's include a few more constraints:)

3) The number of **vowels** and the number of **consonants** must also each be divisible by 7.

   (Getting more challenging? Let's add a few more:)

4) The number of words that **begin with a vowel** must be divisible by 7.

5) The number of words that **begin with a consonant** must be divisible by 7.

    (Let's add some frequency constraints:)

6) The number of words that **occur more than once** must be divisible by 7.

7) The number of words that **occur in more than one form** shall be divisible by 7.

8) The number of words that **occur in only one form** shall be divisible by 7.

    (Now let's add some constraints on the grammatical structure:)

9) The number of **nouns** shall be divisible by 7.

10) Only 7 words shall *not* be nouns.

11) The number of **names** in the genealogy shall be divisible by 7.

12) Only 7 **other kinds of nouns** are permitted.

13) The number of **male names** shall be divisible by 7.

14) The number of **generations** shall be 21, also divisible by 7.

    A challenging assignment, indeed! Could *you* do it?

If you encountered such a genealogy, would you attribute such characteristics as these to random chance?

These have all been met (in the Greek) in the genealogy of Jesus Christ in the first 11 verses of the Gospel of Matthew.

The heptadic (sevenfold) structure of the Bible has been much studied and the subject of numerous volumes in the past,[28] but none are more provocative than the works of Dr. Ivan Panin, to whom we are indebted for these observations.[29]

Chance as the Rival Conjecture?

The difficulties of matching a corpus of any text to fit the numerical rules are staggering. For each feature listed there are six chances of failing and only one of success. For *two* such features at the same time, there is only one in 7 x 7, or 49, chances of "winning." In fact, for each additional feature required, the odds pile up against complete success rather quickly:

For 2:	$7^2 = 7 \times 7$	49
For 3:	$7^3 = 7 \times 7 \times 7$	343
For 4:	$7^4 = 7 \times 7 \times 7 \times 7$	2,401
For 5:	$7^5 =$	16,807
For 6:	$7^6 =$	117,649
For 7:	$7^7 =$	823,543
For 8:	$7^8 =$	5,764,801
For 9:	$7^9 =$	40,353,607

The discussion of the genealogy in Matthew detailed 14 features, several of which were interdependent. The odds of a random text complying to only 9 heptadic constraints is over 40 million to one! (If it took you 10 minutes per draft, and you worked 40 hours a week for 50 weeks per year, it would take over 3,000 years to accomplish this task by random trials!

The Last 12 Verses of Mark

There are some scholars who believe the last 12 verses of Mark were not in the original and were added later. This has become a dispute among many.

(Many Bibles have a footnote to that effect, excessively relying on the Alexandrian codices (4th century) and the writings of Westcott and Hort, et al. It is becoming increasingly understood that these 12 verses were *expurgated* from the Alexandrian codices and were actually in the original. Irenaeus, in 150 AD, quotes them in his commentary, as does Hypolatus in the 2nd century.)

Do you think that a clever scribe could have composed these verses on his own? The passage in question has over 34 heptadic features,[30] which would seem to make their inclusion by human manual methods seem a bit difficult:

$$7^{34} = 54,116,956,037,952,111,668,959,660,849.$$

One million supercomputers, composing 400 million drafts per second, would require over 4 million years to complete that number!

This is with only 34 features. Panin has identified 75!

This heptadic attribute seems to operate as an automatic security monitor–watching over every single letter of the text–that doesn't rust or wear out, and has been standing watch for several thousand years. It is of an uncompromisable design and can be viewed as the "authenticating fingerprint" of the Author Himself.

Vocabulary

One of the simplest–and most provocative–aspects of the Biblical text is the vocabulary used. The number of vocabulary words in a passage is, of course, different from the total number of words in a passage. Some words are repeated. It is easy, for example, to use a vocabulary of 500 words to write an essay of 4,000 words.

There are words in Matthew that *occur nowhere else* in the New Testament. There are 42 such words (7 x 6) and they have 126 letters (7 x 18). Again, always an exact multiple of 7. How could this possibly have been organized?

Even if Matthew contrived to include this characteristic into his Gospel, how could he have known that these specific words–whose sole characteristic is that they are not to be found in the other New Testament books–were *not to be used by the other writers*? If this was the result of a deliberate design on his part, how could he have organized this?

Unless we assume the absurd hypothesis that he had a prior agreement with all of the other writers, he must have had the rest of the New Testament before him when he wrote his book. This characteristic would thus imply that the Gospel of Matthew, then, must have been written *last.*

It so happens, however, that the Gospel of Mark exhibits the *same* phenomena. This, too, suggests that the Gospel of Mark would *also* have had to be written "last."

The same phenomena are found in Luke...and in the writings of John, James, Peter, Jude and Paul. Each would have had to write *after* the other in order to contrive these vocabulary usages! You can thus demonstrate that each of the New Testament books had to have been written "last."

Was this due to "chance" or was it the result of deliberate, skillful design? There is no human explanation for this incredible and precise structure. It appears to have all been supernaturally designed or edited. We simply gasp, sit back, and behold the skillful handiwork of the Ultimate Author.

We are indebted to the painstaking examinations and lifetime commitment of Dr. Ivan Panin for uncovering some of these amazing insights.

Ivan Panin was born in Russia on December 12, 1855. Having participated in plots against the Czar at an early age, he was exiled and after spending some years in study in Germany, came to the United States and entered Harvard University. After graduation in 1882, he converted from agnosticism to Christianity.

In 1890 he discovered some of the phenomenal mathematical designs underlying both the Greek text of the New Testament and the Hebrew text of the Old Testament. He was to devote over 50 years of his life painstakingly—and exhausting his health—exploring the numerical structure of the Scriptures, generating over 43,000 detailed hand-penned pages of analysis. He went on to be with the Lord in his 87th year, on October 30, 1942.

Bibliography:

Missler, Chuck, *How We Got Our Bible*, Koinonia House, 2000.

McCormack, R., *The Heptadic Structure of Scripture,* Marshall Brothers Ltd., London, 1923.

Panin, Ivan, (Various works); write to Bible Numerics, Suite 206, 121 Willowdale Avenue, Willowdale, Ontario Canada, M2N 6A3.

Selection Four

The Value of Pi

I have often been challenged by a skeptic concerning the view that the Bible is inerrant–free from errors (in the original). One of the alleged discrepancies in the Old Testament deals with an item being built for Solomon's Temple by Hiram the Bronzeworker:

> *And he made a molten sea [brazen laver], ten cubits from the one brim to the other: it was round all about, and his height was five cubits: and a line of thirty cubits did compass it round about.*
> 1 Kings 7:23

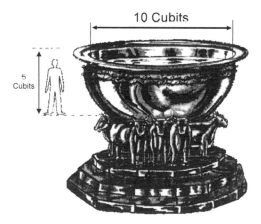

The huge cast bronze basin was 10 cubits[31] in diameter and its circumference is said to be 30 cubits, which is mathematically inaccurate. Any schoolboy knows that the circumference of a circle is *not* the diameter times 3, but rather, the diameter times the well-known constant called π ("Pi"). The real value of π is 3.14159265358979, but is commonly approximated by 3 1/7.

This is assumed, by many, to be an error in the Old Testament record, and so it is often presented by skeptics as a rebuttal to the "inerrancy" of the Scripture. How can we say that the Bible is inerrant when it contains such an obvious geometrically incorrect statement? How do we deal with this?

In this case, the Lord ultimately brought to our attention some subtleties usually overlooked in the Hebrew text.[32]

In Hebrew, it reads:

וַיַּעַשׂ אֶת־הַיָּם מוּצָק עֶשֶׂר בָּאַמָּה מִשְּׂפָתוֹ עַד־שְׂפָתוֹ עָגֹל
סָבִיב וְחָמֵשׁ בָּאַמָּה קוֹמָתוֹ [וּקְוֵה] [וְקָו]
שְׁלֹשִׁים בָּאַמָּה יָסֹב אֹתוֹ סָבִיב:

A Spelling Lesson

The common word for circumference is קָו, *qav*. Here, however, the word seems to be misspelled. Yet, even misspellings can prove deliberate and revealing! The spelling of the word for circumference, קְוֵה, *qaveh*, adds a *heh* (ה). (In the text above each word also has a leading ו as a conjunction for the masculine singular noun.)

In the Hebrew Bible, the scribes never altered any text which they felt had been previously copied incorrectly. Rather, they noted in the margin what they thought the written text should be. The written variation is called a *kethiv,* (here as וּקְוֵה); and the marginal annotation is called the *qere* (here, וְקָו).

To the ancient scribes, this was also regarded as a *remez,* a hint of something deeper. This appears to be a clue to treat the word as a mathematical correction.

Alphanumeric Reckoning

The use of alphanumerics (using the alphabet for numbers) was employed by both the Hebrews and the Greeks. The Hebrew values are listed below:

א	1	ח	8	ס	60	ת	400
ב	2	ט	9	ע	70	ך	500
ג	3	י	10	פ	80	ם	600
ד	4	כ	20	צ	90	ן	700
ה	5	ל	30	ק	100	ף	800
ו	6	מ	40	ר	200	ץ	900
ז	7	נ	50	ש	300		

Numerical Values

Since the Hebrew alphabet is alphanumeric, each Hebrew letter also has a numerical value assigned and can be used as a number. The ק has a value of 100; the ו has a value of 6; thus, the normal spelling of this word would yield a numerical value of 106.

The addition of the ה, with a value of 5, increases the numerical value to 111. This suggests the adjustment to the ratio of 111/106 , which results in 31.41509433962 cubits.

Assuming that a cubit was 1.5 ft.,[33] this 15 foot-wide bowl would then have had a circumference of 47.12388980385 feet. This Hebrew "code" results in 47.12264150943 feet, or an error of less than 15 thousandths of an inch! This error is 15 times *better* than the 3 1/7 estimate that we were accustomed to using in school!

How would they even know this?   This accuracy would seem to vastly exceed the precision of their instrumentation.

Beyond these engineering insights from Solomon's day, there are more far reaching implications of this passage.

1) The Bible *is* reliable. The "errors" pointed out by skeptics usually derive from misunderstandings or trivial quibbles.

2) The numerical values of the letters are legitimate and apparently can carry hidden significance. There are some who maintain that the numerical assignments in the Hebrew alphabet were borrowed from the Greek alphabet in a later period, perhaps from the influence of Pythagoras, and others (580 -500 BC),[34] but this has all been refuted.[35] The Hebrew use of the alphanumeric alphabet clearly predates these assumptions.[36]

Even misspellings can have profound significance. But Christmas is coming. . .

Selection Five

Why a Virgin Birth?

*Behold, a virgin shall conceive, and bear a
son, and shall call his name Immanuel.*

Isaiah 7:14

Every Christmas season we ponder this strange miracle.
There are many profound reasons; this is but one of them.

The Problem

God announced very early that His plan for redemption
involved the Messiah being brought forth from the tribe of
Judah,[37] and specifically from the line of David.[38]

However, the succession of the subsequent kings of Judah
proved to be, with only a few exceptions, a dismal chain. As
the succeeding kings went from bad to worse, we eventually
encounter Jeconiah (also known as Jehoiachin) upon whom
God finally pronounced a "blood curse" on the royal line:

*Thus saith the Lord, Write ye this man childless, a man
[that] shall not prosper in his days: for no man of his
seed shall prosper, sitting upon the throne of David,
and ruling any more in Judah.*

Jeremiah 22:30

This created a rather grim and perplexing paradox: the Messiah had to come from the royal line, yet now there was a curse on that very blood line!

(I always imagine that there must have been a celebration within the councils of Satan on that day. Surely he must have surmised that God was now caught in a quandary. But then I visualize God saying to the angels, "Watch this one!")

The Solution

The solution is revealed in the *different* genealogies of Jesus Christ recorded in the Gospels.

Matthew, as a Levi, focused his gospel on the Messiahship of Jesus and presents Him as the Lion of the Tribe of Judah. Thus, Matthew traces the *legal* line from Abraham (as any Jew would) through David, then through Solomon (the "royal" line, through the first surviving son of Bathsheba) to Joseph, the *legal* father of Jesus.[39]

On the other hand, Luke, as a physician, focused on the *humanity* of Jesus, and thus presents Him as the *Son of Man*. Luke traces the blood line from Adam (the first Man) through to David–and his genealogy from Abraham through David is, of course, identical to Matthew's. But then after David, Luke departs from the path taken by Matthew and traces the family tree through *another* son of David (the second surviving son of Bathsheba), Nathan, which carries it down through Heli, the father of Mary, the mother of Jesus. Joseph is the *son-in-law* of Heli.[40]

Thus, Jesus is "of the house and lineage of David," but not heir to the blood curse pronounced upon the descendants of Jeconiah. The genealogy of Jesus Christ is on the next page:

Luke	Matthew & Luke	Luke	Matthew
		Nathan	Solmon
Adam		Mattatha	Rehoboam
Seth		Menan	Abijah
Enosh		Melea	Asa
Kenan		Eliakim	Jehoshaphat
Mahalalel		Jonan	Jehoram
Jared		Joseph	Ahaziah*
Enoch		Juda	Joash*
Methuselah		Simeon	Amaziah*
Lamech		Levi	Uzziah
Noah		Matthat	Jotham
Shem		Jorim	Ahaz
Arphaxad		Eliezer	Hezekiah
Salah		Jose	Manasseh
Eber		Er	Amon
Peleg		Elmodam	Josiah
Reu		Cosam	Jehoiakim*
Serug		Addi	Jehoiachin*
Nahor		Melchi	Salathiel
Terah		Neri	Zerubbabel
	Abraham	Salathiel	Abiud
	Isaac	Zerubbabel	Eliakim
	Jacob	Rhesa	Azor
	Judah	Joanna	Sadoc
	Pharez	Juda	Achim
	Hezron	Joseph	Eliud
	Ram	Semei	Eleazar
	Amminadab	Mattathias	Matthan
	Nahshon	Maath	Jacob
	Salmon	Nagge	Joseph
	Boaz	Esli	
	Obed	Naum	
	Jesse	Amos	
	David	Mattathias	
		Joseph	
		Janna	
		Melchi	
		Levi	
		Matthat	
		Heli	
		(Mary)	

* Ahaziah, Joash, and Amaziah, all died violent deaths; God thus dealing with idolatry literally "to the 3rd and 4th generations (Exodus 20:4,5), their names therefore "blotted out" according to the Law (Deut 29:20). Jehoiakim and Jechoniah likewise, since the kingdom ended as an independent kingdom with Josiah's death at Megiddo. Thus these were "blotted out" of the groups of "14 generations" in Matthew's account. (Cf. E. W. Bullinger, *Companion Bible,* Appendix 99.)

The Daughters of Zelophehad

There is a peculiar exception recorded in the Torah: the result of a petition by the daughters of Zelophehad, which provided for inheritance through a *daughter* if no sons were available and she married within her tribe.[41] In such cases, the son-in-law was adopted by the father of the bride.[42]

It's remarkable how many commentaries fail to recognize that the inheritance of Jesus through Mary *depends upon this specific exception* deriving from the daughters of Zelophehad. There is nothing trivial or irrelevant in the Bible. Indeed, we discover that *every* detail in the Scripture is there by design and ultimately points to Jesus Christ.

In Chapter 12 we'll explore another. But first, let's now explore the most amazing passage in the Bible!

(This is the passage that so startled me in its implications that it changed my life and my entire concept of reality.)

Selection Six

The Seventy Weeks

*Seventy sevens are determined upon thy
people and upon thy holy city...*

Daniel 9:24

We will now explore what is probably the most
astonishing passage in the entire Bible. It will demonstrate
the incredible precision with which the Bible details "history
in advance," thus authenticating its origin from outside our
time domain.

The Key to our own Future

This passage *also* holds the key to understanding the
period emerging on the horizon just ahead of us. We are
presently being thrust into the period of time about which the
Bible says more than it does about any other period of time
in history—including the time that Jesus walked the shores of
Galilee and climbed the mountains of Judea. And the key to
understanding end-time prophecy is in this very passage.

Four disciples came to Jesus privately for a confidential
briefing about His Second Coming. His response was so
important that it is recorded in three of the four Gospels.[43] In
this briefing, Jesus highlighted this very passage in Daniel
Chapter 9 as the key to understanding the times.[44]

The Book of Daniel was part of the Old Testament, and, as such, was translated into Greek in 270 B.C. as part of the Septuagint translation of the Hebrew Scriptures. Although Daniel is one of the most authenticated books of the Bible, this simplifying observation will serve to establish the *undeniable existence* of the book long before the events it so precisely predicts.

Daniel had been deported as a teenager and then spent the next 70 years in captivity in Babylon. He was reading the prophecies of Jeremiah[45] from which he understood that the 70-year period of captivity which had been predicted was coming to an end, and so he then committed himself to prayer. During his prayer, the angel Gabriel interrupted him and gave him the most remarkable prophecy in the Bible. The last four verses of Daniel Chapter 9 are this famed "Seventy Week Prophecy of Daniel." It will behoove us to examine this passage *very carefully*.

The Seventy Weeks

The last four verses of Daniel 9 also outline the fourfold structure of the passage:

9:24	The scope of the entire prophecy;
9:25	The 69 Weeks (of years);
9:26	An Interval between the 69th & 70th Week
9:27	The 70th Week

(The key to understanding this passage is to recognize that the 70 "Weeks" are not all contiguous, and that verse 26 includes an explicit *interval between* the 69th and 70th Weeks.)[46]

Verse 24: The Scope

> *Seventy weeks are determined upon thy people and upon thy holy city, to finish the transgression, and to make an end of sins, and to make reconciliation for iniquity, and to bring in everlasting righteousness, and to seal up the vision and prophecy, and to anoint the most Holy Place.*   Daniel 9:24

Seventy *shabu'im* ("sevens," or "weeks") speaks of weeks of years. This may seem strange to us, but the Hebrew traditions include a week of days, a week of weeks (*shavout*), a week of months,[47] and a week of years.[48] Seventy sevens of years are determined, or "reckoned" (*hatak*), upon Daniel's people and the city of Jerusalem. Notice that:

1) The focus of the passage is on the *Jews*, not the Church nor the Gentile world. Also,
2) There are six major items which have *yet to be completed*:
   1) to finish the transgressions;
   2) to make an end of sins;
   3) to make reconciliation for iniquity;
   4) to bring in everlasting righteousness;
   5) to seal up (close the authority of) the vision;
   6) to anoint the *Godesh Godashim,* the Holy of Holies.

(The fact that all of these have not yet been fulfilled in 2,000 years also demonstrates that the time periods *are not contiguous*.)

360 Day Years

All ancient calendars were based on a 360-day year: the Assyrians, Chaldeans, Egyptians, Hebrews, Persians, Greeks,

Phoenicians, Chinese, Mayans, Hindus, Carthaginians, Etruscans, Teutons, etc. All of these calendars were based, typically, twelve 30 day months.

In ancient Chaldea, their calendar was based on a 360-day year and it is from this Babylonian tradition that we have 360 degrees in a circle, 60 minutes to an hour, 60 seconds in each minute, etc.

In 701 B.C., all calendars seem to have been reorganized.[49] Numa Pompilius, the Second King of Rome, reorganized the original calendar of 360 days per year by adding five days per year. King Hezekiah, Numa's Jewish contemporary, reorganized the Jewish calendar by adding a month in each Jewish leap year (on a cycle of 7 every 19 years[50]).

In any case, the Biblical calendar, from Genesis to Revelation, uses a 360-day year.[51]

Verse 25: The 69 Weeks

Know therefore and understand, that from the going forth of the commandment to restore and to build Jerusalem unto the Messiah the Prince shall be seven weeks, and threescore and two weeks: the street shall be built again, and the wall, even in troubled times.

Daniel 9:25

The city of Jerusalem, at the time this was received, was in ruins, but destined to be rebuilt. Thus, Gabriel gave Daniel a mathematical prophecy:

$(7 + 62)$ times 7 times $360 = 173,880$ days.

The Seventy Weeks of Daniel

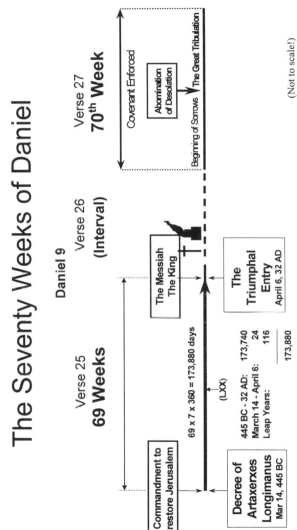

Daniel 9

Verse 25
69 Weeks

Verse 26
(Interval)

Verse 27
70ᵗʰ Week

Covenant Enforced

Abomination of Desolation

The Great Tribulation

Beginning of Sorrows

The Messiah The King

The Triumphal Entry
April 6, 32 AD

69 x 7 x 360 = 173,880 days

(LXX)

445 BC - 32 AD: 173,740
March 14 - April 6: 24
Leap Years: 116
173,880

Commandment to restore Jerusalem

Decree of Artaxerxes Longimanus
Mar 14, 445 BC

(Not to scale!)

(Why the 69 weeks was separated into 7 and 62 remains a point of scholastic conjecture. It has been suggested that seven weeks of years was the duration of the Temple being rebuilt.)

173,880 days would occur between the commandment to rebuild Jerusalem until the presentation of the *Meshiach Nagid.* The initiating trigger, the authority to rebuild the city of Jerusalem, was the decree of Artaxerxes Longimanus, given on March 14, 445 B.C.[52] (There were several decrees concerning the rebuilding of the Temple, but only one that granted the authority to rebuild the walls of the *city*.)

The milestone to complete the 69 weeks was the presentation of the *Meshiach Nagid*, the Messiah the King.[53] But when was Jesus ever presented as a *King?* On several occasions in the New Testament, when they attempted to make Jesus a King, He invariably declined, saying, "Mine hour is not yet come."[54] Then one day, He not only permits it, He *arranges* it.[55]

The Triumphal Entry

Jesus deliberately arranged to fulfill the ancient prophecy which Zechariah had recorded 500 years earlier:

Rejoice greatly, O daughter of Zion; shout, O daughter of Jerusalem: behold, thy King cometh unto thee: he is just, and having salvation; lowly, and riding upon an ass, and upon a colt the foal of an ass.

Zechariah 9:9

This was the *only day* He allowed Himself to be proclaimed as a King.[56] The enthusiastic disciples were declaring Jesus as the Messiah by singing Psalm 118.[57] The

Pharisees expressed their concern since the crowd, in its enthusiasm, was, in their view, blaspheming by thus proclaiming Jesus as the "Messiah the King." Jesus then declared:

> *"I tell you that, if these should hold their peace, the stones would immediately cry out."*   Luke 19:40

This occurred on the 10th of Nisan,[58] or April 6, 32 A.D.[59] When you convert the Hebrew text into the terms of our calendar, we discover that there were *exactly 173,880 days* between the decree of Artaxerxes and the presentation of the "Messiah the King" to Israel! Gabriel's prophecy, given to Daniel five centuries before–and translated into Greek three centuries before the fact–was fulfilled to the *exact Day!*

The Best Bargain in Israel

When you visit Israel, there will be many vendors trying to sell you souvenirs, etc. Your guide will invariably take you to the Mount of Olives for the spectacular photo opportunity of the Old City, the Temple Mount, and the related sites. Typically, your tour will walk down this same road on which Jesus rode the donkey on that fateful day. The Garden of Gethsemane is at the base of this road and that is the usual next stop for most tours.

As you walk down the road, pick up a stone or two and put them in your pocket. When you return home, have someone mount it on an attractive block of wood to display it like a trophy in your living room, study, or office. When someone curiously asks, "What is that?", you can then simply reply, "That's one of the stones that didn't cry out." And then, of course, you will have to explain about Daniel 9, Luke 19, et al. After all, *they* brought it up!

National Blindness Predicted

What is also shocking is that Jesus *held them accountable to recognize this day.* It was this national rejection that led Christ to declare a national blindness that we observe continuing even to this day

> *If thou hadst known, even thou, at least in this thy day, the things which belong unto thy peace! but now they are hidden from thine eyes.* Luke 19:42

The rise of Talmudic Judaism—with its emphasis on human commentary—has replaced the previous commitment to the original text itself, and has thus obscured—and replaced—the Messianic recognition that seems so obvious to the unbiased, diligent inquirer.[60]

Are these things "hidden" (or blinded from Israel) forever? No. Paul tells us how long:

> *For I would not, brethren, that ye should be ignorant of this mystery, lest ye should be wise in your own conceits; that blindness in part is happened to Israel, **until** the fulness of the Gentiles be come in.*
> Romans 11:25

"The fulness of the Gentiles come in?" Where? This appears to be a reference to the controversial issue of the ἁρπάζω, *harpazo*, the "snatching up," or "rapture," of the church.

(This is from 1 Thessalonians 4:17, where the Greek verb signifies to catch up, take by force, catch away, pluck, to seize, carry off by force, to seize on, claim for one's self eagerly, to snatch out or away.[61] In the Latin Vulgate translation, it was translated *rapiemur*, from *rapturo*, from which we derive the common label, the "rapture" of the church–that is, the collecting of the believers in Christ.)

This corporate, or national "blindness" of Israel is thus predicted to endure until after the sudden and mysterious removal of Christ's own. And an entire global scenario of strange and terrifying events will ultimately result in Israel's awakening to the realities of their long awaited Messiah.[62]

The Destruction of Jerusalem Foretold

Jesus went on to predict that Jerusalem would be destroyed *because* they didn't recognize this specific day that Daniel had predicted:

> *For the days shall come upon thee, that thine enemies shall cast a trench about thee, and compass thee round, and keep thee in on every side, And shall lay thee even with the ground, and thy children within thee; and they shall not leave in thee one stone upon another;* [Why?] ...*because thou knewest not the time of thy visitation.*   Luke 19:43-44

38 years after Jesus declared this, the Fifth, Tenth, Twelfth and Fifteeenth Roman Legions, led by Titus Vespasian, laid a seige upon Jersusalem which resulted in over one million men, women, and children being slaughtered.[63]

During the battle, a torch thrown through a window started a fire inside the Temple. The extensive gold furnishings and fixtures melted and Titus had to order every stone taken down to recover the gold. Thus, the specific words of Jesus were fulfilled in the Fall of Jerusalem in 70 AD.

Why was Jerusalem destroyed in 70 AD? There are many answers, but the one Jesus gave is the most provocative: "...because thou knewest not the time of thy visitation." He held them accountable to know the prophecy that Gabriel had given Daniel.

But Gabriel's disclosure to Daniel went even further.

Verse 26: The Interval

And after threescore and two weeks shall Messiah be cut off, but not for himself: and the people of the prince that shall come shall destroy the city and the sanctuary; and the end thereof shall be with a flood, and unto the end of the war desolations are determined.   Daniel 9:26

Verse 26 deals with events *after* the 62 weeks (therefore, also after the earlier seven, thus making it *after* the total of 69 weeks), and yet *before* the 70th week begins, which will be subsequently dealt with in verse 27. It is important to recognize that there are specific events specified *between* the 69th and 70th week, and, thus, not all the weeks are contiguous.

One of the events is that the Messiah shall be "cut off" (*karat*, execution; death penalty). It comes as a surprise to many to discover that the Old Testament *predicts* that the Messiah of Israel was to be *executed*.[64]

Other events that intervene between the 69th and 70th week include the destruction of both the city and the sanctuary. Indeed, just as Jesus had predicted, after the end of the 69th Week, under Titus Vespasian the Roman legions destroyed the city and the sanctuary in 70 AD.

While these specific events have required at least 38 years between the 69th and 70th Weeks of Daniel, this interval has now lasted almost 2,000 years thus far.[65] This interval is that period of national blindness for Israel[66] which Jesus announced. It is also the period that includes the Church (used here in its mystical or spiritual sense rather than in any organizational sense), a mystery kept hidden in the Old Testament.[67]

(It appears that the Lord deals with Israel and the Church *mutually exclusively.* A chess clock, with its two interlocked but mutually exclusive presentations, is an illustrative example: one clock is stopped while the other is running.)

The evidence is accumulating that this interval may be about over, and the famed "70th Week" may be about to begin.

There is one remaining verse which details the final "Seventieth Week" of this prophecy. This seven year period is the most documented period of time in the entire Bible. Many scholars believe that the Book of Revelation, from Chapters 6 through 19, are simply a detailing of this terrifying period on the earth.

This astonishing anticipation of such precise historical details is one of the most dramatic demonstrations of the extraterrestrial origin of the Biblical text. There is no other way to account for it. We are indebted to the classic work of Sir Robert Anderson, a former head of Scotland Yard, for these insights.[68]

Bibliography

Anderson, Sir Robert, *The Coming Prince,* Hodder & Stroughton, London, 1895. Also available in modern versions.

Missler, Chuck, *The Seventy Weeks of Daniel,* Koinonia House, 1993.

Missler, Chuck, *Expositional Commentary on Daniel*, Koinonia House, 1993. (Audio commentaries on tape cassettes or CD-ROMs, with 200 pages of notes, diagrams and references.)

Selection Seven

Child Sacrifice?

Abraham's offering of Isaac on Mount Moriah has puzzled many for centuries. Is God ordaining child sacrifice? Or is there another profound secret hidden behind this strange narrative?

Rhetorical Devices

The Biblical text declares that a variety of rhetorical devices have been included in the text:

I have also spoken by the prophets, and I have multiplied visions, and used similitudes, by the ministry of the prophets.   Hosea 12:10

Of particular significance in studying the Bible are similes, metaphors, allegories, parables and types. A *simile* is a comparison by resemblance; a *metaphor* is a comparison by representation; an *allegory* is a continued metaphor or continued representation; a *parable* is a continued resemblance.

(Sometimes a parable is instructional; however, surprisingly, other times a parable is employed to *restrict* the communication to the specially initiated, excluding those "outside" the circle of initiates.[69])

Macrocodes

In computer programming, macrocodes are employed to express–and thus implement–the anticipatory or structural aspects of a program; macrocodes typically *anticipate* how a series of forthcoming elements are to be laid out, or related to one another.

Often in a word processing application, macrocodes (called "macros") are used to anticipate a *template* for a letter, or a fax, or special report form. They convey a structural intent not necessarily evident without them. They often are used to lay out a composite design, the fonts to be used, special instructions to the printer, etc.

Some of the most important insights can result from perceiving the broader application of an event or *series* of actions in the record. One of the most profound forms of communication is a macrocode, often called a *type*, a figure used to portray something in the future; a foreshadowing; an anticipation of the *antitype*.[70]

In our common vernacular, we often use a "model." If we plan a house, particularly one with multiple levels, we often construct a model first to facilitate the visualization of space and other relationships. In modern engineering, we frequently use mathematical computer models to explore the implications of a design, etc. We also will develop a precedent *prototype* before finalizing a design. *Types* in Biblical texts are the designation for an anticipatory "model" of a future event or person. Some of these are among the most astonishing aspects of the Biblical Scriptures.

We will examine the most classic of these here. We will explore some lesser known ones in Chapter 13.

The *Akedah*

Perhaps the most startling example of a "type" is the famed incident of Abraham offering his son Isaac in Genesis Chapter 22, called in Hebrew, the *Akedah.*

> 2] *And [God] said, Take now thy son, thine only son Isaac, whom thou lovest, and get thee into the land of Moriah; and offer him there for a burnt offering upon one of the mountains which I will tell thee of.*

This is a strange call. Does God hereby endorse child sacrifice? Hardly! But then, what *is* going on? This episode has confused some scholars for centuries.

> 3] *And Abraham rose up early in the morning, and saddled his ass, and took two of his young men with him, and Isaac his son, and clave the wood for the burnt offering, and rose up, and went unto the place of which God had told him.*

By the time Abraham gets to Genesis 22, he has learned many lessons. Notice that he doesn't dally; he starts on his journey the very next morning!

Notice also that there are *four* going on the trip: Abraham, Isaac, and two young men, as well as the donkey.

> 4] *Then on the third day Abraham lifted up his eyes, and saw the place afar off.*
> 5] *And Abraham said unto his young men, Abide ye here with the ass; and I and the lad will go yonder and worship, and come again to you.*

It took 3 days to get to the place now known as Mount Moriah. Notice also that the two young men remain at the base of the hill as the father and son climb up it. (Is Abraham's prediction about both of them returning just a stall, or is it a prophecy?)

The Topology of Mount Moriah

On a following page is a topographical map of Mount Moriah. Mount Moriah is a ridge system between the Mount of Olives to the east and Mount Zion to the west. It is bounded by the Kidron Valley on the east, the Tyropean Valley on the west, and the Hinom Valley to the south.

The ridge begins at the south at about 600 meters above sea level and rises to a peak as one goes northward. At the base of this ridge was the town of Salem at which Melchizedek was both the king and the priest.[71] This later becomes Ophel, the city of David, and ultimately, Jerusalem.

Higher on the ridge, at about 741 meters above sea level, is a saddle point where Ornan later owned a threshing floor, which would eventually be purchased by David to become the site of Solomon's Temple.[72]

(A threshing floor was not necessarily at the peak; it was typically a saddlepoint which enjoyed a prevailing wind which could be used to separate the chaff from the grain when threshed at harvest times.)

The peak of the Mount is a bit further north, at about 777 meters above sea level, at a place which would later become known as Golgotha–*the exact spot where Jesus Christ would be crucified as the offering for sin 2,000 years later.*[73]

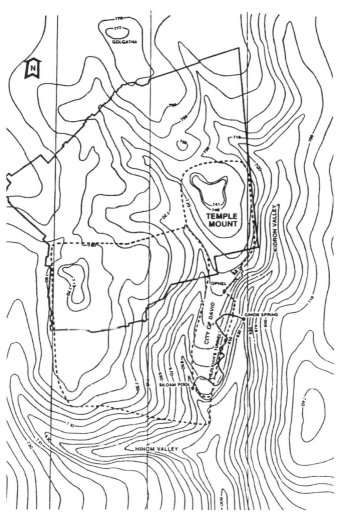

Topographical Map of Mount Moriah

As we begin to understand the *typology* of this narrative, we begin to appreciate the subtleties in the account. Abraham had an earlier son, Ishmael, but for God's purposes here, Isaac is viewed as "your only son."[74]

Careful students of the Scripture have noted The Law of First Mention: that the first occurrence of a word in the Scripture is usually a very significant instance in the overall design. It is profoundly significant that this account includes the first occurrence of the word *love* in the Scripture.[75]

> 6] *And Abraham took the wood of the burnt offering, and laid it upon Isaac his son; and he took the fire in his hand, and a knife; and they went both of them together.*
> 7] *And Isaac spake unto Abraham his father, and said, My father: and he said, Here am I, my son. And he said, Behold the fire and the wood: but where is the lamb for a burnt offering?*

Good question, Isaac. You can appreciate the lad's concern. Notice Abraham's response:

> 8] *And Abraham said, My son, God will provide himself a lamb for a burnt offering: so they went both of them together.*

"God will provide" *who?* Himself! Was this also just a stall? Did Abraham realize that he was acting out a prophecy? *Two thousand years later–on that very spot–another Father would offer His Son as the offering of all time!*

> 9] *And they came to the place which God had told him of; and Abraham built an altar there, and laid the*

wood in order, and bound Isaac his son, and laid him
on the altar upon the wood.

We are all victims of our Sunday School coloring books:
we always picture Isaac as a small boy. Some scholars
maintain that Isaac was about 30 years old.

10] *And Abraham stretched forth his hand, and took
the knife to slay his son.*

11] *And the angel of the LORD called unto him out of
heaven, and said, Abraham, Abraham: and he said,
Here am I.*

12] *And he said, Lay not thine hand upon the lad,
neither do thou any thing unto him: for now I know that
thou fearest God, seeing thou hast not withheld thy son,
thine only son from me.*

13] *And Abraham lifted up his eyes, and looked, and
behold behind him a ram caught in a thicket by his
horns: and Abraham went and took the ram, and
offered him up for a burnt offering in the stead of his
son.*

Thus, we encounter the substitutionary ram. When Adam
and Eve "fell" in the Garden of Eden, even then, God taught
them that by the shedding of innocent blood they would be
covered.[76] All of the Levitical sacrifices in the Torah were
designed to anticipate the climactic sacrifice for all time, also
foreshadowed here. We are the beneficiaries of a love story,
written in blood on a wooden cross, which was to be erected
in Judea some two thousand years later.

14] *And Abraham called the name of that place
Jehovah-jireh: as it is said to this day, In the mount of
the LORD it shall be seen.*

Abraham then gave the location a *prophetic* label. It appears that he somehow *knew* that he was acting out a prophecy!

Abraham also knew that Isaac, if offered, would have to be resurrected since God had previously promised Abraham that Isaac would have numerous descendants.[77] (It is interesting that Isaac was "dead" to Abraham for three days: from the time the commandment came until he was freed by the angel.)

Here, in this "type," or macrocode, we have Abraham cast in the role of the Father and Isaac as the Son. The ultimate drama of God the Father offering His Son are the referrents or designata to which this historical narrative appears to be alluding. There is even another subsequent example in which, again, the roles, or referrents, are the same.

A Bride For Isaac

Later, in Genesis 24, Abraham commissions his "eldest servant" to gather a bride for Isaac, who then travels to the designated place, qualifies the woman (Rebecca) by a well, and offers her the opportunity to marry the bridegroom she has never seen; and she accepts. She ultimately meets her bridegroom at the Well of *LaHai-Roi*, the "Well of the Living One [who] sees me."

Here, again, Abraham is a "type" of the Father; Isaac, the Son; and Rebecca, his bride, suggestive of God's specially chosen, the Church.[78]

The designation "Eldest Servant" is misleading to us: he was Abraham's business partner and would have inherited all Abraham possessed if Abraham had not had any issue. He is cast, here, as a type of the Holy Spirit, called to gather the bride for Isaac. He is not named here, but we know from previous passages that his name was Eleazer, which means "Comforter."[79]

A Textual Omission?

Returning to our earlier review of Genesis 22, immediately after the substitutionary offering, we come to verse 19:

19] *So Abraham returned unto his young men, and they rose up and went together to Beersheba; and Abraham dwelt at Beersheba.*

Notice that in the list of who came down from the mountain to return home, only Abraham and the two young men at the bottom of the hill are listed. *Where's Isaac?*

Naturally, we infer that Isaac also joined them and that there were four who traveled back to Beersheba. But that's *not* what the text says! It seems that Isaac has disappeared: the person of Isaac has been *edited out of the record*, from the time that he is offered on the mount *until he is united with his bride*, two Chapters later![80] It would seem that the text has been subtly tailored so as to fit the broader design, to be consistent with the larger picture; a type–or macrocode–highlighting the climax to come.

We will be exploring some larger "macrocodes" in Chapter 13. In the next Chapter we will encounter an even higher perspective by consolidating some numerical data.

Selection Eight

Signs of the Heavens

The heavens declare the glory of God;
and the firmament sheweth his handywork.

Psalm 19:1

In Numbers chapters 1 and 2, we encounter the census of the people and the detailed instructions for their encampment. Why? What hidden insight lies behind them?

Of course, there are many valid historical reasons for the inclusion of these details in the Torah (the five books of Moses). But our premise is that there isn't any detail included that isn't there by deliberate design. If we examine these details more closely, some remarkable insights emerge.

The Tabernacle

When Moses received the Ten Commandments on Mt. Sinai, he also received detailed specifications and instructions for the building of a portable sanctuary, the Tabernacle, or Tent of Meeting.[81] The purpose of this unusual facility was to provide a place for God to dwell among His people.[82]

The Tabernacle was always set up at the center of the Camp of Israel, facing eastward. The tribe of Levi was assigned to care for it, and encamped around it. Moses,

Aaron, and the priests camped on the east side next to the entrance. The three families of the tribe of Levi (Merari, Kohath, and Gershon), camped on the north, south, and west side, respectively. The remaining Twelve Tribes were grouped into four camps around the Levites.

A Baker's Dozen

It is helpful to realize that there were really 13 tribes, not just "twelve." This can be confusing to the uninitiated reader.

Jacob had twelve sons, each becoming the founder of one of the Twelve Tribes. However, Joseph was sold into slavery and subsequently emerged as the prime minister of Egypt.[83] In Egypt, Joseph married Asenath and had two sons, Manasseh and Ephraim. When Jacob and the rest of the family ultimately joined them in Egypt, Jacob adopted his two grandsons as his own.[84] With the tribe of Joseph then in two parts, we have an "alphabet" of 13 to choose from.

The Twelve tribes of Israel (Jacob) are listed twenty times in the Old Testament. [85] They are listed by mother (Leah, Rachel, Zilhah, and Bilhah), their numeration, their encampment, order of march, their geographical relations, etc. Each time they are listed in a different order.

The Levites were exempt from military duties. When the order of military march is given, there are still 12 listed, *excluding* Levi. This is accomplished by dividing Joseph into two: Ephraim and Manasseh.

(Levi is thus omitted on four occasions. In a similar manner, Dan is omitted on three occasions, the most notable one in Revelation 7.)

The Mazzeroth

The Hebrew name for the zodiac is the *Mazzeroth*.[86] The ancient Hebrew names hold the key to the original designations of the constellations that were later corrupted at the Tower of Babel and that continue even to today.[87]

It is amusing to see planetarium shows still spreading the notion that the various pictures associated with the constellations were ancient imaginings taken from the *arrangement* of the stars. If you have carefully explored that conjecture, it is easily discarded as fanciful and absurd. Have you ever tried to visualize the "bear" in *Ursa Major*, known more commonly as the "Big Dipper"? Or tried to "see" a "lady chained to a chair" in the bent-W known as *Cassiopeia*?

The key to the original concepts lying behind the various "signs" were the *names of the stars* associated with each sign, in their order of magnitude (brightness). The names of the stars recounted a story, summarized in the name and the associated picture of each "sign." These were convenient mnemonics (aids to memory) to recalling and teaching the overall narrative. Ancient Persian and Arabic traditions ascribe the invention of astronomy to Adam, Seth, and Enoch.

The narrative, beginning at the Virgin *(Virgo)*, continues around the Zodiac to climax with the Lion of the Tribe of Judah (Leo). Deciphering these "cosmic macrocodes" depends upon discovering the ancient Hebrew names of the stars involved. Unfortunately, many are no longer available, but Arabic, Aramaic, and similar traditions are suggestive.

Each of the Twelve Tribes of Israel were associated with one of the 12 constellations.[88] Let's take one example:

Virgo

Virgo is traditionally pictured as a woman with a branch in her right hand and an ear of corn in her left. Named from the Latin for virgin, in Hebrew she is called *Bethulah*, a virgin.

The brightest star is *Spica*, an ear of corn.[89]   In Hebrew, it is *Zerah*, the Seed (the "Seed of the Woman").[90]   In Egyptian, it is *Aspolia*, the seed.

The second brightest is, in Hebrew, *Tsemech*, the Branch, a title of the Messiah.[91]   Other stars include *Zavijaveh*, gloriously beautiful;[92] and *Al Mureddin*, who shall have dominion.[93]

It is significant that the Sign of Virgo is also associated with the tribe of Zebulun, where Nazareth is located.[94]

The Four Faces

Each time we encounter a view of the Throne of God, we notice the same strange living creatures–some kind of "SuperAngels"–somehow associated with the protection of His throne, His holiness, etc. We also notice the same four faces: a Lion, a Man, an Ox, and an Eagle.[95] We will also encounter them in a key role among the tribal standards of the Twelve Tribes of Israel.

There are some who notice the specific focus of each of the four Gospels–Matthew, Mark, Luke, and John–is centered around four themes: The Messiah, the Lion of the tribe of Judah; The Suffering Servant; The Son of Man; and the Son of God, respectively. It has been noted that the four faces are not inappropriate to symbolize the four Gospels.

The Four "Camps"

The Twelve Tribes, excluding the Levites, were grouped into four "camps."[96] Each of these groups, of three tribes each, were to rally around the tribal standard of the lead tribe.

Judah's tribal standard was, of course, the lion. Reuben's ensign was a man; Ephraim's the ox; Dan's, ultimately, the eagle. It is interesting to note that these four primary tribal standards - the lion, the man, the ox, and the eagle - are the same as the four faces of the strange living creatures ("Super Angels?") that always appear surrounding the Throne of God.[97]

It would seem that the camp of Israel - with the tabernacle in the middle - would, thus, appear to be a model of the Throne of God: His presence in the center (represented by the tabernacle), encircled by the four faces, this all surrounded by His people.

But there's even more. Why the specific numbers?

The Census

The numbering of the tribes is detailed in Numbers Chapter one. The actual population represented is obviously somewhat larger than these enumerations, since only men over twenty and able to go to war, were counted. Most analysts assume that women, children, and the elderly, would multiply the count factor by 3 or whatever. The total camp would thus appear to approximate two million.

While the numbers of each tribe may not seem very revealing, the totals for each of the four camps will be:

Judah	74,600	Reuben	46,500
Issachar	54,400	Simeon	59,300
Zebulun	57,400	Gad	45,650
	186,400		151,450
Ephraim	40,500	Dan	62,700
Manasseh	32,200	Asher	41,500
Benjamin	35,400	Naphtali	53,400
	108,100		157,600

Cardinal Compass Points

Each of the camps, of three tribes each, were to encamp on one of the four cardinal compass directions (N, S, E, or W) with respect to the camp of the Levites enclosing the Tabernacle.[98] We can only guess at how much space was required by the Levites, whether it was 100 ft. on a side, 100 yards, or whatever. But whatever it was, we'll assume that length as a basic unit.

To fully appreciate all of the implications, you must try to think like a rabbi: you need to maintain an extremely high respect for the precise details of the instructions. They resorted to heroic measures in their attempt to comply with the letter of the law.

The tribes of Judah, Issachar, and Zebulun–collectively called the Camp of Judah–had to encamp *east* of the Levites. This poses a technical problem. Notice that if the breadth of their camp was larger than that of the Levites, the excess would be southeast or northeast, *not east*. Therefore, if they were to strictly comply with their instructions, their camp could only be as wide as that of the Levites, and they then would have to extend *eastward* to obtain the required space.

The camps of Reuben, Ephraim, and Dan had the same constraint on the south, west, and north respectively. The length of each leg would thus be proportional to the total population in each camp.

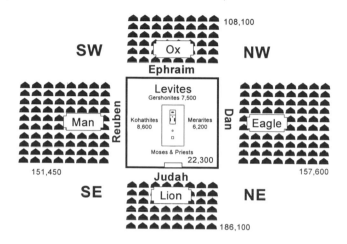

The Aerial View

If we assemble what we can infer from the Torah account, we can imagine what the camp of Israel looked like from above: the Tabernacle and the Levites in the center, surrounded by the four faces of the tribal standards, and each of the four camps of Judah, Ephraim, Reuben, and Dan, stretching out in the four cardinal directions.

We can also tally the approximate size of each tribe to determine the *relative* length of each camp as they stretched out in each of the four cardinal directions. The startling results are on the next page.

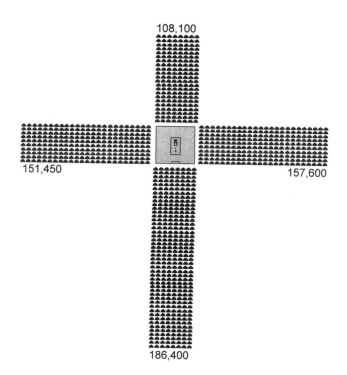

It would appear that when the Israelites encamped, they formed a giant cross! This is a graphic macrocode, indeed! And this is from the Torah, not the New Testament!

The New Testament is, indeed, in the Old Testament concealed; the Old Testament is in the New Testament revealed.

Addendum: More on the *Mazzeroth*

Each of the 12 constellations of the *Mazzeroth* are associated with three additional constellations called decans.

The three constellations (decans) that are associated with Virgo are *Coma* (the Desired One), *Centaurus* (the Despised One), and *Bootes* (the Coming One).

Coma is, in Egyptian, *Sheznu*, the Desired Son.[99] It is usually depicted as a woman with an infant. (What is a woman with an infant doing in the sign of a virgin?)

Centaurus in Hebrew is *Bezeh*, the Despised One.[100] Another name in Hebrew is *Asmeath*, the sin offering.[101] In the Greek traditions there is the name *Cheiron,* which means the Pierced One.[102] One of the stars is, in Hebrew, *Toliman* which means here, before, and hereafter, similar to the identity given in the Burning Bush, the "I Am."[103]

Bootes, the Coming One,[104] includes the principal stars of *Arcturus*, He cometh;[105] *Al Katuropos*, the branch that is trodden under foot; *Mirac*, preserver, guarding; *Muphride*, he who separates and *Nekkar*, the Pierced One.[106]

Notice the dual nature: God, and yet despised. The double nature is imbedded in the idea of the sin offering of the despised one at the same time being the ultimate ruling King. In 1893 we found out that the star *Tsemech* in Virgo is a double star!

Bibliography for the Mazzeroth:

Missler, Chuck, *Signs in the Heavens*, Koinonia House 1991.

Bullinger, E. W., *The Witness of the Stars*, Kregel Publications, Grand Rapids MI, 1967 (reprint of London edition, 1893).

Seiss, Joseph A., *The Gospel in the Stars*, Kregel Publications, Grand Rapids MI, 1972 (reprint of *Primeval Astronomy*, 1882).

Spencer, Duane Edward, *The Gospel in the Stars*, Word of Grace, San Antonio TX, 1972.

Allen, Richard H., *Star Names, Their Lore and Meaning*, Dover Publications, New York 1963 (Republished from Stechert, 1899).

Kunitzsch, Paul, and Smart, Tim, *Modern Star Names and Their Derivations*, Harrassowitz, Wiesbaden, 1986.

Bibliography for the Camp of Israel :

Fruchtenbaum, Arnold G., *Israelology: the Missing Link in Systematic Theology,* Ariel Press, Tustin CA, 1989.

Missler, Chuck, *Expositional Commentaries on Genesis, Revelation,* Koinonia House, Coeur d'Alene, ID, 1995.

Selection Nine

At the Foot of the Cross

For many scholars, the most majestic–and most Messianic–book of the Old Testament is the Book of Isaiah. The majesty of its language, and the sweep of its vision, is unequaled anywhere. And the high point of this book is the famed 53rd Chapter, called by many, "the Holy of Holies" of the Old Testament text.

The Old Testament passage presents the Messiah of Israel as the Suffering Servant and includes a description and role of the crucifixion that is without equal in the entire Bible. The clarity of the prophetic presentation of Chapter 53 of Isaiah is so anticipatory of the New Testament message, that some of the Ashkenazi Jews had this passage removed from their Scriptures. (However, the Sephardic Jews retained it.)

When the Dead Sea Scrolls were discovered in 1947, among the most prized treasures included was a complete scroll of Isaiah, and guess what was right there in the middle of it: Chapter 53. You can see it for yourself when you visit Jerusalem in the specially built Shrine of the Book which is adjacent to the Israeli Museum.

In addition to the *Great Isaiah Scroll*, dating from about 100 B.C., fragments representing another 21 copies were found. The scroll was one which might have been in use at the very time that Jesus opened His public ministry by reading from an Isaiah scroll in the synagogue in Capernaum.[107] Furthermore, since it was a copy, it may have reflected a text that went back to within only a generation or so of the prophet Isaiah himself.[108] When a comparison was made between the *Isaiah Scroll* and the classic Masoretic Text, it became evident that the two were almost identical, even though the Qumran text was more than six centuries older than the text of the Masoretes![109]

Rabbi Yakov Rambsel has observed how the complete phrase, *Yeshua shmi*, ישוע שמי, "Jesus is my name," appears hidden uniquely behind the text in the key passage of Isaiah 53.[110] This phrase occurs *only here*, and appears to clearly endorse the identity of the Servant portrayed in the text.

But the simple presence of the name *Yeshua* is not where it ends. Rabbi Rambsel has made the startling discovery that not only Jesus Christ, but *over forty names of individuals and key places appear to be encoded behind this critical text.*

Before we explore some of the specific details, it would be good to examine the famous passage of Isaiah 53 itself. (It is widely recognized that the thrust of this remarkable passage actually begins at Isaiah 52:13, as below:)

Behold, my servant shall deal prudently, he shall be exalted and extolled, and be very high. As many were astonied at thee; his visage was so marred more than any man, and his form more than the sons of men: So shall he sprinkle many nations; the kings shall shut their mouths at him: for that which had not been told them shall they see; and that which they had not heard shall they consider. Who hath believed our report? and to whom is the arm of the LORD revealed? For he shall grow up before him as a tender plant, and as a root out of a dry ground: he hath no form nor comeliness; and when we shall see him, there is no beauty that we should desire him. He is despised and rejected of men; a man of sorrows, and acquainted with grief: and we hid as it were our faces from him; he was despised, and we esteemed him not. Surely he hath borne our griefs, and carried our sorrows: yet we did esteem him stricken, smitten of God, and afflicted. But he was wounded for our transgressions, he was bruised for our iniquities: the chastisement of our peace was upon him; and with his stripes we are healed. All we like sheep have gone astray; we have turned every one to his own way; and the LORD hath laid on him the iniquity of us all. He was oppressed, and he was afflicted, yet he opened not his mouth: he is brought as a lamb to the slaughter, and as a sheep before her shearers is dumb, so he openeth not his mouth. He was taken from prison and from judgment: and who shall declare his generation? for he was cut off out of the land of the living: for the transgression of my people was he stricken. And he made his grave with the wicked, and with the rich in his death; because he had done no violence, neither was any deceit in his mouth. Yet it pleased the LORD to bruise him; he hath put him to grief: when thou shalt make his soul an offering for sin, he shall see his seed, he shall prolong his days, and the pleasure of the LORD shall prosper in his hand. He shall see of the travail of his soul, and shall be satisfied: by his knowledge shall my righteous servant justify many; for he shall bear their iniquities. Therefore will I divide him a portion with the great, and he shall divide the spoil with the strong; because he hath poured out his soul unto death: and he was numbered with the transgressors; and he bare the sin of many, and made intercession for the transgressors.

Isaiah 52:13 - 53:12

This is an astonishing passage in its own right. It is unequaled in its clarity of presentation of the crucifixion of Christ. The details included summarize the New Testament presentation in undeniable terms, even though it was penned over 700 years before the events transpired. And it was part of the Septuagint translation completed in the third century *before Christ was born.* And the apparent codes certainly would not have been tailored into the text by any rabbis, even if they could have!

With this background, let's review a few of the remarkable discoveries which appear to lie encrypted behind the text itself.

The label "Nazarene," (*Netzer,* נזיר) is also a well-known identity of Jesus.[111] While this term appears a dozen times in the Book of Isaiah, it seems significant that it, too, appears here in this key Messianic passage. The term *Galilee* also appears twice.[112] As isolated events, these "encoded" labels don't seem that significant. But appearing in *combination*, they seem to rise above any ambient noise level.

The time of Passover, the location of Mount Moriah, and the names of Herod and Caesar also seem to make their appearance. Both of the names of Annas and Caiaphas, the high priests,[113] also appear. Annas was the former high priest and the uncle of Caiaphas. Both of them figure prominently in three of the six trials endured by Jesus following the arrest in Gethsemane.[114]

The most startling discovery has been the names of essentially all of the disciples and the others who were at the foot of the cross that fateful afternoon. While the specific names involve relatively frequent combinations of letters individually, their appearance *in combination*, and their relevance to the text, would seem to argue against their occurring by unaided chance alone.

The name of Peter (*Kepha,* כפה) appears in Isaiah 53:3, beginning with the second letter of the fifth word and counting every nineteenth letter from right to left. With over 300 occurrences in the Book of Isaiah, this incidence in isolation wouldn't seem especially significant; but the coincidences are piling up.

The name of John (*Yochanan,* יוחנן) also appears in Isaiah 53:10, starting with the fourth letter in the eleventh word and counting every 28th letter from left to right. This is a bit more significant since this code appears only nine times in the entire Book of Isaiah. There are some other aspects to the specific location that will be discussed shortly.

The name of Andrew (*And'drai,* אנדרי) appears in Isaiah 53:4, beginning with the first letter of the eleventh word, counting every 48th letter from left to right (in reverse). Since there are only five such occurrences in the entire Book of Isaiah, its appearance here compounds the evidence against this all occurring by unaided chance alone.

The name of Philip (*Pilip,* פילף) also appears in the passage. Since there are only 15 such appearances in the entire Book of Isaiah, its inclusion in this cluster adds additional weight to the inference of deliberate design.[115]

Thomas (*Toma,* תומא) also appears in Isaiah 53:2, starting with the first letter in the eighth word and counting every 35th letter from right to left. As there are over 200 appearances of this code in the Book of Isaiah, in isolation this doesn't seem that compelling; but, again, clustering with the others they collectively are seen to be rising above any residual noise level.

Simon (Zelotes), the Canaanite, (*Shimon,* שמעון) appears in Isaiah 52:14, beginning with the first letter in the second word and counting every 47th letter from right to left. With only 15 such occurrences in the entire Book, its inclusion here seems significant.

Thaddaeus (*Taddai,* תדי) appears in Isaiah 53:12, beginning at the first letter of the eighth word and counting every 50th letter from left to right. (This high frequency combination appears nine times in this passage and would be deemed to have little relevance on its own. Again, it's the composite collective appearances that appear profoundly significant.)

The Two Jameses

The name James (the English equivalent of the Greek *Jacobus,* or the Hebrew *Ya'akov* יעקב) appears twice behind the text, at intervals of -20 and -34 (that is, in reverse). James, or *Ya'akov*, was a common name in that period.[116] What makes this double occurrence particularly provocative, however, is that there were apparently *two* Jameses present at the Cross.

One of them was James, the son of Zebedee[117] and the brother of John,[118] with whom he was called by Jesus to be one of the Twelve.[119] Jesus nicknamed James and John "Boanerges," meaning "sons of thunder."[120] These two are very prominent in the various lists of the Twelve,[121] and were clearly on the inside circle. With Peter, they were present when Jesus raised Jairus's daughter,[122] at the Transfiguration,[123] at a confidential briefing on Jesus' Second Coming,[124] and were with Jesus in the Garden of Gethsemane.[125] James was among the first martyrs by decapitation at the command of Herod Agrippa I.[126]

The other James was the son of Alphaeus, another of the twelve apostles.[127] He is usually identified as "James the younger."[128]

There was also a third James, *who apparently was not present at the cross.* He was the Lord's half-brother, who, along with his brothers Joses, Simon and Judas,[129] apparently did not accept the authority of Jesus before His resurrection.[130] After the risen Jesus had appeared to him,[131] James became a leader of the Jewish-Christian church at Jerusalem.[132] A few years later James suffered martyrdom by stoning at the instigation of the high priest Annas during the interregnum after the death of the procurator Festus in AD 61.[133]

It is interesting that the name James appears to be encoded precisely twice in this critical text.

The Three Marys

Mary (*Miryam,* מרים) was also a relatively common name in that period, and there were three Marys at the cross with John:

> Now there stood by the cross of Jesus his mother, and his mother's sister, Mary the wife of Cleophas, and Mary Magdalene.
> When Jesus therefore saw his mother, and the

*disciple standing by, whom he loved, he saith unto his
mother, Woman, behold thy son!*
   *Then saith he to the disciple, Behold thy mother! And
from that hour that disciple took her unto his own home.*
                                                    John 19:25-27

Grant Jeffrey has noted that in Isaiah 53:11, starting with
the fifth letter in the ninth word and counting every 20th letter
from left to right spells *Ma 'al Yeshua Shmi ohz,*
מעל ישוע שמי עז: "exceedingly high, *Yeshua* is my strong
name."[134] (It is this *yod* (י) in *Yeshua's* name that is the same
letter that encodes *Yochanan,* John, noted earlier.)

In Isaiah 53:11, beginning with the first letter in the first
word and counting every 42nd letter from left to right spells
"Messiah," *Meshiach* משיח. From the *mem,* מ, in the word
"Messiah," counting every 23rd letter from left to right spells
"Mary," מרים. In Isaiah 53:10, all three Marys use the letter
yod (י) in the word, *ya'arik* יאריך. This is the same letter *yod*
(י) that forms the first letter of the encoded names "*Yeshua*"
and "John." Despite the fact that the combination of letters
which make up Mary, מרים, are extremely frequent (there are
over 11,000 in the Old Testament, over 600 in Isaiah and over
a dozen in this passage), it is this intimate interlinking of the
three Marys with both *Yeshua* and John that is rather striking.

There are over 40 relevant names in 15 sentences. It is the
density, *and the relevance to the plaintext,* which would seem
to defy attribution to unaided random chance alone.

Here is a summary of some of the codes that Rabbi Yakov Rambsel and Grant Jeffrey have reported.[135]

Name		*Begins*	*Word*	*Letter*	*Interval*
Yeshua is my name	ישוע שמי	53:10	11	4	-20
His Signature	מחתימו	53:7	8	4	49
Messiah	משיח	53:11	1	1	-42
Nazarene	נזיר	53:6	11	3	47
Galilee	גליל	53:7	1	2	-32
Shiloh	שילה	53:12	21	4	19
Pharisee	פרוש	53:9	14	2	-64
Levites	לוים	54:3	3	6	19
Caiaphas	כיפה	53:15	7	3	41
Annas	ענן	53:3	6	5	-45
Passover[136]	פסח	53:10	13	3	-62
The man Herod	איש הורד	53:6	4	1	-29
The Evil Roman City	רע עיר רומי	53:9	13	2	-7
Let Him be crucified	יצלב	53:8	6	2	15
Moriah[137]	הירמ	52:7	4	5	153
Cross	צלכ	53:6	2	2	-8
Pierce	דקר	53:10	15	3	-92
The Atonement Lamb	מכפר טלא	52:12	12	2	-19
The Disciples mourn	למדים אנן	53:12	2	3	-55
Peter	כפה	53:10	11	5	-14
Matthew	מתתי	53:8	12	1	-295
John	יוחנן	53:10	11	4	-28
Andrew	אנדרי	53:4	11	1	-48
Philip	פילף	53:5	10	3	-133
Thomas	תומא	53:2	8	1	35
James	יעקב	52:2	9	3	-34
James	יעקב	52:2	3	4	-20
Simon	שמעון	52:14	2	1	47
Thaddaeus	תדי	53:12	9	1	-50
Matthias	מתיה	53:5	7	4	-11
Mary	מרים	53:11	1	1	-23
Mary	מרים	53:10	7	3	6
Mary	מרים	53:9	13	3	44
Salome[138]	שלמית	52:15	16	3	113
Joseph	יוסף	53:2	1	2	210
Bread[139]	הלחם	53:1	1	8	210
Wine	יין	53:5	11	2	210

An Ominous Omission

There is also a surprising *omission* among the names apparently encrypted in Isaiah 53: יהודה, Judas. This combination of letters appears over fifty times in Isaiah and yet does *not* appear in Isaiah 53. His replacement, Matthias, (*Mattiyah*, מתיה), however, *does* appear.[140]

So the controversy over the ELS codes continues.

An Instructive Example

Consider very carefully the following seemingly innocuous paragraph:

> "Upon this basis I am going to show you how a bunch of bright young folks did find a champion: a man with boys and girls of his own; a man of so dominating and happy individuality that Youth is drawn to him as is a fly to a sugar bowl. It is a story about a small town. It is not a gossipy yarn; nor is it a dry monotonous account, full of such customary "fill-ins" as "romantic moonlight casting murky shadows down a long, winding country road." Nor will it say anything about twinklings lulling distant folds; robins carolling at twilight, nor any "warm glow of lamplight" from a cabin window. No. It is an account of up-and-going activity; a vivid portrayal of Youth as it is today; and a practical discarding of that worn-out notion that 'a child don't know anything.'"

Did you notice anything unusual about this paragraph? Examine it carefully and see if you can perceive an astonishing characteristic before reading any further.

There is not a single *e* in this passage! Would you attribute this unusual characteristic to random chance? Hardly. (Try composing even a single sentence yourself without using a letter *e*.)

The science of cryptology depends heavily on the statistical behavior of language. For example, the expected frequency of *e*'s, in English, is around 13%, with a ±2% deviation well within the range expected by chance. (It was sensitivity to this frequency distribution of the English alphabet that led to Samuel Morse's design of his familiar Morse Code: the high frequency *E* is simply a single dot; *T*, a single dash; etc.)

What would you conclude if you were to discover that this paragraph was excerpted from a complete novel without a single *e* in it? Would you attribute *that* to coincidence or to the result of deliberate, skillful, diligent effort?

The quoted paragraph comes from a 267-page book entitled, *Gadsby, A Story of Over Fifty Thousand Words Without Using the Letter E*, published in 1939 by Ernest Vincent Wright.[141] The author's perseverance in his self-imposed task is a tale in itself. He could never use *the* or the pronouns *he, she, they, we , me* and *them*. He could not use the such seemingly indispensable verbs as *are, have, were, be,* and *been*. He couldn't use such basic words as *there, these, those, when, then, more, after* and *very*. He actually had to tie down the *e* bar of his typewriter to make it impossible for one to slip in.

The comparable task of authenticating a series of messages by encoding relevant codes within the message itself, while maintaining the sense and validity of the narrative enclosing it, represents an even more prodigious task than simply the avoidance of the use of any individual letter. (By contrast, the ELS codes do appear to be a dynamic, multilevel, interactive, Cardano grille, designed not to conceal but rather to reveal and authenticate.)

Res ipsa loquitur. "The thing speaks for itself," as some lawyers might conclude.

But are the ELS codes real?

To the skeptics, these are all simply chance occurrences deriving from the density and lack of redundancy of the Hebrew text. To the proponents of the codes, they appear as astonishing confirmations of the supernatural origin of the text. It is not as simple as it first seems.

The difficulty lies in that the ELS codes appear, to most, to fall somewhere in between: they are too provocative to dismiss; yet not definitive or systematic enough to fully accept. Much more careful and skillful research remains to be done.

The ELS codes appear to be only relevant if they do, in fact, reveal attributes beyond the capabilities of human authorship. The strange discoveries in Israel may eventually prove to be contributions to the most significant scientific research that has ever been undertaken. They would appear to confirm the view that precisely 50 days after the Exodus from Egypt, that the Torah was dictated directly to Moses in a precise letter-by-letter sequence. And if these codes are valid, and portray events occurring in the future when received, the Source of this dictation would have to come from outside our domain of spacetime. Furthermore, the continuing intervention throughout the centuries implies a supernatural stewardship that also demands our serious attention.

It must be kept in mind that coincidental codes have been claimed for any long segment of text, even in English. The skeptics point out, with substantial validity, that the ELS codes are facilitated by the nature of the Hebrew language, and its density due to the shorter alphabet and its absence of vowels. This is especially true for *Yeshua*, יֵשׁוּעַ, which has only four letters, two of which, the *yod*, י, and the *wav*, ו, are the most common in Hebrew.

The rebuttal to the criticism that Hebrew lends itself to such word play is that, perhaps, it was *designed* for this very purpose.[141]

The rebuttal to ELSs being simply a chance phenomena are their occurrence behind relevant plaintext, the clustering of related codes, and the absence of significant alternative candidate names within the cluster.

*   *   *

For Further Reading:

Missler, Chuck, *Cosmic Codes - Hidden Messages From the Edge of Eternity,* Koinonia House, 1999.

Jeffrey, Grant, *The Handwriting of God*, Frontier Research Publications, Toronto, Ontario, Canada, 1997.

Yacov Rambsel, *His Name is Jesus*, Frontier Research Publications, Toronto, Ontario, Canada, 1997.

Selection Ten

The Once and Future Calendar

The Jew's catechism is his calendar.
–Samson Raphael Hirsch

We all know the story of Noah's Flood, and how God wiped out the entire Planet Earth to make a new beginning. (The reasons for this drastic action are too complex to explore in this brief review.[143]) Having provided for Noah and his family by means of the fabled ark, the end of the Flood is recorded rather specifically:

> *And the ark rested in the seventh month, on the*
> *seventeenth day of the month, upon the mountains of*
> *Ararat.* Genesis 8:4

If you are a normal, well adjusted, reader, when you encounter this verse you simply read on. But if you have been to one of my Bible studies, you are no longer a normal, well adjusted reader! You will recall my emphasizing that the entire Bible–the 66 books, penned by over 40 authors over thousands of years–constitute an *integrated message system*, and there is nothing trivial in it: every detail is there by *deliberate* design. So you might ask yourself, why did the Author want you to know that the new beginning on the Planet Earth began on the 17th day of the 7th month?

The mystery begins to unravel as we examine the details of the Jewish calendar.

The Feasts of Israel

The Torah–the five books of Moses–details seven feasts during the Hebrew calendar.[144] The first three feasts are celebrated in the Spring, in the month of Nisan: Passover (*Peshach*), Feast of Unleavened Bread *(Hag HaMatzah)*, and the Feast of First Fruits. (Colloquially, these are all connotatively included in the celebration of Passover.)

Fifty days later there is the Feast of Weeks, *Shavout*, also known as Pentecost ("50"). It was celebrated the day following the "counting of the omer" (49 days + 1), 50 days after the Feast of First Fruits.

There are three remaining feasts in the fall, in the month of Tishri: the Feast of Trumpets (*Yom Teruah*); the Day of Atonement, *(Yom Kippur)*; and the Feast of Tabernacles (*Succoth*).

While each of these feasts has an historical commemorative role, they also each have a *prophetic* role. When God set their feast times, the very terms He used are suggestive: מוֹעֵד, *mowed*, which means "to keep an appointment," and מִקְרָא, *mikraw*, which means "rehearsal."[145] Paul emphasized this[146] and also highlighted their predictive role as "a shadow of things to come."[147] Jesus also pointed to his personal role in their fulfillment:

> *Think not that I am come to destroy the law (Torah), or the prophets: I am not come to destroy, but to fulfil.*
> Matthew 5:17

Passover

The celebration of Passover commemorates the deliverance of Israel from the bondage of Egypt,[148] spoken of there as God's "firstborn."[149] This deliverance had been predicted to Abraham 430 years earlier.[150]

The climax of the series of plagues which God sent upon the Egyptians was the death of the firstborn.[151] The blood of the lamb sacrifice was put on the doorposts on that fateful eve, so that the Angel of Death would "pass over" the house. (It was the blood, not their nationality, that delivered the house from the terrifying judgment. Even this detail anticipates the love letter which was written in blood on a wooden cross erected in Judea over a thousand years later.)

This "passing over" was reckoned as "between the evenings" of the 14th of Nisan on the Jewish calendar, in which each new day begins at sundown. On the Egyptian calendar, however, this was still Friday the 13th, a grim day from the Gentile point of view, which continues to cast its shadow in various superstitions even to this very day.[152]

The Jews were instructed to commemorate their deliverance from that day forward and it still remains as one of the most significant observances in their national life. The details of this observance are very instructive.

The lambs to be sacrificed were to be presented for inspection on the 10th of Nisan, and were to be slain "between the evenings" of the 14th. Nothing was to be left to the next day.[153] And, interestingly, "not a bone was to be broken."[154]

Messianic Fulfillment

Entire books have been written on the numerous details of the various feasts which appear to have been fulfilled in the New Testament. None are more dramatic than those associated with the Feast of Passover.

When John first introduced Jesus publicly, twice he announced, "Behold the Lamb of God that taketh away the sin of the world."[155] This is a very Jewish label. Paul also describes Jesus as "our Passover."[156]

As we explored in Chapter 6, Jesus presented Himself on the 10th of Nisan, the very day that the lambs were being presented for inspection at the Temple. He was deemed "without blemish,"[157] and the personal representative of the ruler of the world declared, "I find no fault in him."[158]

It is also interesting that, contrary to the instructions from their military commander, the soldiers exempted Him from the breaking of the bones which had been ordered to hasten the otherwise lengthy process.[159] Victims of crucifixion have been known to take many days to expire; so in deference to the impending holidays, the process was to be completed before sundown; "between the evenings."

The shedding of His blood was also anticipated in His last supper with the disciples in the giving of wine.[160] In the traditional Passover observance, there are four cups, labeled: "Bringing out," "Delivering," "Redemption or Blessing" and "Taking Out." Apparently it was with the *third* cup that Jesus administered the communion,[161] and then He said,

> *But I say unto you, I will not drink henceforth of this*
> *fruit of the vine, until that day when I drink it new with*

you in my Father's kingdom. Matthew 26:29

This supper is regarded by some scholars as yet to be completed upon His return. It is interesting that the fourth cup is called the "Taking Out."

In present day Judaism, the Passover wine is mixed with warm water.[162] Why?

But when they came to Jesus, and saw that he was dead already, they brake not his legs: But one of the soldiers with a spear pierced his side, and forthwith came there out blood and water. John 19:33, 34

It is also interesting that even the language of the Lord in the Torah hints that this was (to be) done "unto me":

*And thou shalt shew thy son in that day, saying, This is done because of that which the LORD did **unto me** when I came forth out of Egypt.* Exodus 13:8

Feast of Unleavened Bread

Closely associated with Passover–and commonly regarded as part of the same observance—was *Hag haMatzah,* the Feast of Unleavened Bread.[163] It was one of the three feasts distinguished by the compulsory attendance of every able-bodied male Jew.[164]

In order to understand the Levitical practices, it is important to recognize that leaven was symbolic of sin. It seems to be an unusually apt metaphor since it "corrupts by puffing up," and the source of all sin is pride.[165] This symbol (or code) is *consistently* used in the Old Testament[166] and in the New.[167]

Part of the Passover observance, even today, is the *Bedikat hametz*: the ritual search for leaven in the home. A small amount is usually "hidden" for the children to discover as part of the family observance.[168]

It is interesting that the *Matzah*, the unleavened bread used in the Passover observance, has stripes and is pierced.[169] There are three, and the middle one is broken, wrapped in a cloth and hidden. Isn't that suggestive?

> *Then were there two thieves crucified with him, one on the right hand, and another on the left.* Matthew 27:38

> *And when Joseph had taken the body, he wrapped it in a clean linen cloth, And laid it in his own new tomb, which he had hewn out in the rock: and he rolled a great stone to the door of the sepulchre, and departed.*
> Matthew 27:59, 60

These "codes," or metaphors, such as the "unleavened bread," are intriguingly consistently applied throughout the Scriptures. Jesus also declared, "I Am the Bread of Life."[170] This can also be linked to the provision of the manna during Israel's wanderings in the wilderness,[171] and other relevant incidents.

The bread and wine together, as anticipatory "codes," are also seen when Melchizedek, as priest of the Most High God, received tithes from Abraham and then administered bread and wine.[172]   When Joseph was cast into prison, he encountered these same elements when confronted with the dreams of the baker and the wine steward.[173] It is interesting that "three days" are also part of the mystical imagery, and that the bread baker was "broken," while the wine led to Joseph being ultimately redeemed.

The more one carefully examines the Old Testament narratives and declarations, the more evident is the skillful and deliberate inclusion of "macrocodes" detailing events–and their significance–in the distant future. These evidences are both irrefutable authentication of their extraterrestrial origin and are inexhaustible in their import. (We will examine several more in Chapter 13.)

Feast of First Fruits

The Feast of First Fruits is generally regarded as simply a harvest celebration, but it contains some startling hidden surprises. It was, indeed, to celebrate a harvest, but it also looks forward to a harvest of a very different kind.

This unique observance was to occur "on the morning after the Sabbath" after Passover.[174] There was a particular Sunday morning that, while the smoke was curling heavenward from the Temple offerings of the Feast of First Fruits, a group of disciples were discovering an empty tomb.[175]

But there's more.

The Two Calendars of Israel

The Jewish "New Year"–Rosh Hoshana, the "head of the year"–is celebrated in the fall, on the 1st of Tishri. However, when God established the Passover, He also instructed Moses to make Nisan, in the Spring, "the beginning of months":

This month shall be unto you the beginning of months: it shall be the first month of the year to you.

Exodus 12:2

Thus, the Jews have two calendars: their traditional civil calendar starting in the fall, in their month of Tishri, and their religious calendar beginning in the spring, in the month of Nisan. In Genesis we are still using the traditional Jewish calendar which begins in the month of Tishri. It isn't until the Book of Exodus that we have the "new" religious calendar instituted.[176] What is the "seventh" month?

Months	Old	New
Tishri, (Ethanim)	1	7
Cheshvan, (Bul)	2	8
Chisleu	3	9
Tevet	4	10
Sh'vat	5	11
Adar	6	12
Nisan, (Aviv)	**7**	**1**
Ilyar (Zif)	8	2
Sivan	9	3
Tammuz	10	4
Av	11	5
Elul	12	6

So the "seventh month" of Genesis, the month of Nisan, becomes "beginning of months" in Exodus.

Christ was crucified on Passover, specified to occur on the 14th of Nisan, becoming "our Passover." How long was Jesus in the grave? 3 days.[177] 14 + 3 = 17. The day of His resurrection was, thus, the 17th day of the "seventh" month.

Thus, God arranged for His "new beginning" of the Planet Earth in the days of Noah to occur on the "anniversary"–in advance–of our "new beginning" in Christ! How's that for calling your shots in advance!

Selection Eleven

The First and the Last

This is an interesting identity that God uses of Himself:

*...I the Lord, **the first, and with the last**; I am he.*
                                          Isaiah 41:4

*Thus saith the Lord the King of Israel, and his redeemer the Lord of hosts; **I am the first, and I am the last**; and beside me there is no God.*   Isaiah 44:6

*Hearken unto me, O Jacob and Israel, my called; I am he; **I am the first, I also am the last**.*   Isaiah 48:12

This identity is continued in the Book of Revelation:

*Saying, I am Alpha and Omega, **the first and the last**...*
                                          Revelation 1:11

*I am Alpha and Omega, the beginning and the end, **the first and the last**...*   Revelation 22:13

"The First and the Last" is, thus, also expressed in the New Testament as the "Alpha and Omega," which are the first and last letters of the Greek alphabet. These are also continued as an identity:

*I am **Alpha and Omega**, the beginning and the ending, saith the Lord, which is, and which was, and which is to come, the Almighty.*   Revelation 1:8

*And he said unto me, It is done. I am **Alpha and Omega**, the beginning and the end. I will give unto him that is athirst of the fountain of the water of life freely.*
Revelation 21:6

This identity is clearly the Jesus of the New Testament as further clarified in Revelation 1:17 & 18:

*I am **the first and the last**: I am he that liveth, and was dead; and, behold, I am alive for evermore, Amen; and have the keys of hell and of death.*

And also in Revelation 2:8:

*These things saith **the first and the last**, which was dead, and is alive...*[178]

Much to the chagrin of those who promote doubts as to this identity, this is clearly the Lord Jesus Christ.

An Untranslated Word?

In the Old Testament there is an interesting passage in Zechariah 12:10:

And I will pour upon the house of David, and upon the inhabitants of Jerusalem, the spirit of grace and of supplications: and they shall look upon me whom they have pierced, and they shall mourn for him, as one mourneth for his only son...

This passage is remarkable since it presents, 500 years in advance, the Messiah of Israel as the "One Whom They Have Pierced," an allusion to the crucified Messiah.[179]

It is even more remarkable when one examines the *Hebrew* text. Below is an excerpt from a Hebrew Interlinear Bible, in which the English translation for each word is just below it. (But remember, the Hebrew goes from right to left. All nations write toward Jerusalem: all nations east of Jerusalem, write from right to left; all nations west of Jerusalem write from left to right. Curious, isn't it?)

וְהִבִּיטוּ	אֵלַי	אֵת	אֲשֶׁר־	דָּקָרוּ
they And	on me	↕ ?	whom	have they pierced
look shall				

Notice that there is an *untranslated* word between the "me" and the "whom." It is simply two letters, the *aleph* and the *tau*, the first and last letters of the Hebrew alphabet. The *aleph* can signify the first in a list or rank; the *tau*, the last, or completing, element in a list or rank.

This would seem to suggest a more insightful translation could be:

....*and they shall look upon me*, **the Aleph and the Tau,** *whom they have pierced...*

This would be the Hebrew equivalent of the Greek, "Alpha and Omega."[180]

It should also be noted that the אֵת is normally used as a grammatical element to indicate a direct object, so this example is viewed by many skeptics as coincidental or contrived. However, the Greeks had many prepositions, but

the Hebrews had few.   Hebrew prepositions in the Old
Testament have many various meanings which had to be
inferred from the context. [When את is used to indicate a
direct object, it is usually accompanied by a *maqqeph*, a kind
of "connector dash," which bonds two words together into a
single unit.] There are also instances, however, where את is
used as an indefinite *pronoun*; where it is used as a pronoun
to indicate the 2nd person masculine singular; where it is used
to mean a ploughshare; and other applications.

This could also be an idiomatic use of a preposition[181]–a
grammatical pun, if you will, or more precisely, a
hypocatastasis (from the Greek for "putting down
underneath," designates a hidden but declarative implied
metaphor, expressing a superlative degree of resemblance).[182]
That, indeed, appears to be its function in the passage
above![183]

We find the similar thing occurs in Genesis 1:1.

בְּרֵאשִׁית	בָּרָא	אֱלֹהִים	אֵת	הַשָּׁמַיִם	וְאֵת	הָאָרֶץ:
In the beginning	created	God	(?)	the heaven	and	the earth

In the beginning God, (את), created the heaven and the
earth.

Again we have the same two letters, the *aleph* and the *tau*.
In fact in Genesis 1 you will find the *aleph* and the *tau*, *seven*
times, in the process of creation.   Again, it is generally
assumed to relate to the grammatical structure, or it could be
a hypocatastasis, amplifying the identity of the Creator.

In any case, the attribution of the Creation to Jesus Christ is confirmed in several Scriptures,[184] notably in the opening verses of John's Gospel:

> *"In the beginning was the Word, and the Word was with God, and the Word was God. The same was in the beginning with God. All things were made by him and without him was not anything made that was made."*
>
> John 1:1-3

Created by whom? By *Jesus Christ*. "The Word" (λόγος, *Logos*) is one of His titles. One could call it the "code name" of the Author! (It is interesting that the "Creator" title is one suggestive of the information sciences.) It is only when we comprehend who Christ *is* that the Bible really begins to make sense.

> *"And in him was life and the life was the light of men. And the light shineth in the darkness and the darkness comprendeth it not."*   John 1:4, 5

This is the ultimate code which we all desperately need to "decipher." *Just who is He?*

The Heavens declare His glory...
   and the firmament shows His handiwork...
He who is, who was, and who always will be;

The first and the last
   He is the Alpha and Omega
      the Aleph and the Tau
         the A and the Z;

He is the ἐγώ εἰμί, (*ego eimi*);
   the אֶהְיֶה אֲשֶׁר אֶהְיֶה (*ichyach asher ichyach*);
     the "I AM that I AM"!
        ...the voice of the burning bush;

...the Captain of the Lord's Host, the conqueror of Jericho

"He was crucified on a cross of wood;
   Yet He made the hill on which it stood!"

By Him were all things made that were made;
   Without Him was not anything made that was made;
     And by Him are all things held together.

It wasn't the nails that held him to that tree:
   (At any time He could have said, "I'm out of here!")
     It was His love for you and me.

He was born of a woman so that we could be born of God;
He humbled Himself so that we could be lifted up;
He became a servant so that we could be co-heirs;
He suffered rejection so that we could become His friends;
He denied Himself so that we could freely receive all things;
He gave Himself so that He could bless us every way;

His name is above every name;
   That at the name of *Yeshua*
     Every knee shall bow,
        Every tongue shall confess,
           That Jesus Christ is Lord!

His is the kingdom, and the power, and the glory
     for ever, and ever. Amen?

Selection Twelve

The Cities of Refuge

Though he slay me, yet will I trust in him...
Job 13:15

I have long insisted that everything in the Bible is there by specific design, and, further, relates, somehow, to Jesus Christ. I have been challenged on this view: "Aren't some of the Biblical rules and regulations simply quaint tribal customs?"

We have already explored the peculiar exception granted to the daughters of Zelophehad in Chapter 5. Another specific challenge was the strange practice involving the "Cities of Refuge."

The Cities of the Levites

After the conquest of Joshua was completed, the land of Canaan was divided, by lot, among the Twelve Tribes.[185] (As we pointed out in Chapter 8, there were actually 13 tribes.) The tribe of Levi, however, did not inherit land as "the Lord was their inheritance."[186] They were, however, awarded 48 cities, six of which were designated "cities of refuge."[187]

If someone was killed by an assailant, his slayer would be pursued by the next of kin, the *goel*, the avenger of blood. In the case where there was no premeditation–what we would term "manslaughter,"–the slayer could seek refuge in the nearest city of refuge. Assuming that he could convince the elders at the gate of the city that there was no premeditation, etc., he was secure from the avenger of blood, *as long as he remained within the city.* If the slayer left the confines of the city of refuge, he was fair game to the avenger of blood.[188]

All of this remained in this state until the death of the high priest in Jerusalem. After the death of the high priest the slayer was free to leave the city of refuge, free of any further jeopardy from the avenger of blood.

In Israel they had no police force, or prisons. Still, it does seem like a strange procedure. The fate of the slayer was dependent upon his ability to access the nearest city of refuge.

And what has the death of the high priest, in distant Jerusalem, have to do with any of this? Why should this impact the status of the fugitive refugee?

Quaint Rule or Spiritual Insight?

These peculiar arrangements are expressly specified in the Torah, the most venerated part of the Old Testament. Paul emphasized,

> *For whatsoever things were written aforetime were written for our learning, that we through patience and comfort of the scriptures might have hope.* Romans 15:4

"Whatsoever things" means everything. What's the possible *spiritual* significance behind this unusual procedure involving the cities of refuge?

Jesus also declared,

> *The volume of the book is written of me.*
> Psalm 40:7; (q.v. Hebrews 10:7)

So, perhaps, the key to any Biblical dilemma is to put Jesus right into the middle of it and see what emerges! (In fact, that can also apply to any of the issues of life!)

First or Second Degree?

Let's begin by examining the death of Jesus Christ. Was it "first degree" (premeditated) murder or "second degree " (manslaughter)?

From God's point of view, it was "first degree." It was ordained "being delivered by the determinate counsel and foreknowledge of God,"[189] and, thus, from the Father's point of view, it was indeed premeditated. In fact, it was a deal struck with the Son before the foundation of the world!

Our Predicament

But what about *our* position? After all, it *was* our sins which put Him on that cross! Would this be considered "first" or "second" degree murder?

Remember the words of Jesus Himself, (who is, after all, our own defense counsel): "Father, forgive them; for they know not what they do."[190] I would argue that, for this purpose at least, it could be considered manslaughter, and would qualify us to flee to our city of refuge!

And just where *is* our city of refuge? In *Jesus Christ Himself*, of course.

I am crucified with Christ: nevertheless I live; yet not I, but Christ liveth in me: and the life which I now live in the flesh I live by the faith of the Son of God, who loved me, and gave himself for me.   Galatians 2:20

For the law of the Spirit of life in Christ Jesus hath made me free from the law of sin and death.

Romans 8:2

And all this was to obtain until the death of the high priest. Who is *our* High Priest? Jesus Christ.[191]

And it was His death that has freed us from the pursuit of the Avenger of Blood.[192]

However, every check, to be cashed, requires an endorsement of the recipient.   Every pardon needs an acceptance. Have *you* laid claim to what He has purchased for *you*?

We are all victims of the cesspool of deceit of this world and our genetic defect of sin. Yet *He* is the Way, the Truth, and the Life. And He is waiting to hear from you. There is an "800 number" on the 24-hour hotline to the Throne Room of the Universe and He is anxious for you to call!

Why not use it right now?

Selection Thirteen

Strategic Macros

Macrocodes

The use of macrocodes in a message series can result in a form of higher level redundancy which can overcome "noise," errors, distortions, and even enemy countermeasures, by conveying the overall strategic perspective over a broader horizon. These can also serve to confirm or validate the message and its source.

In a series of message segments, the evidence of macrocodes can also reveal the broader intent of the designer of the series. As we stand further back from the artist's canvas, the overall design becomes evident, which can confirm the strategic plan, and overall structure, and can provide a supplemental perspective which validates our perceptions of the artist's intent.

It is the use of Biblical macrocodes which are *chronologically anticipatory* that reveal that the source of a message is extraterrestrial–i.e., from outside our spacetime. In fact, it is this exploitation of this extratemporal characteristic of the message series that is used by the Source to authenticate its origin. He alone knows the end from the beginning.[193]

The Book of Ruth as a Macrocode

One cannot really comprehend what is going on in Revelation Chapter 5 unless one understands the events involved in the Book of Ruth in the Old Testament. This tiny four-chapter romance has been venerated in college classes for its elegance as literature, but it also reveals a craftsmanship of prophetic anticipation unrivaled anywhere in Scripture.

The narrative involves a hero, Boaz, who is in the role of a *goel*, or Kinsman-redeemer, whose ultimate commitment of redemption returns forfeited land in Bethlehem to its disenfranchised former owner, Naomi, and who also takes a Gentile bride, Ruth.

To follow the plot, one must understand the Law of Redemption. Remember that in ancient Israel, land wasn't sold in *fee simple*,[194] as we are used to. Since God was the landowner, Israel was simply a tenant under conditions of obedience. When land was "sold," what the buyer received was only the *use* of the land, not clear title. There were conditions under which a kinsman of the seller could "redeem" the land back to the original family. These conditions were typically noted on the outside of the scroll defining the transaction.[195]

The scroll in Revelation Chapter 5 was written "within and on the backside." The Kinsman of Adam, in His role as Redeemer, is taking possession of what He had already purchased with His blood as the sacrificial Lamb. He not only purchased the land; he also purchased a Bride.

In the Book of Ruth, Naomi is in the role of Israel, exiled

from her land; Boaz is her kinsman who performs the redemption; and Ruth (a Gentile) is also *purchased* for a wife.[196] This "macrocode" extends to virtually every detail of the book. It is interesting that Ruth is introduced to Boaz through an unnamed servant. The Gentile bride is introduced to the ultimate kinsman-redeemer by the Holy Spirit here, too, as an unnamed servant.

It is interesting that Ruth learns how to deal with this situation from Naomi, just as we learn of God's plan of redemption through His dealings with Israel. It is also provocative that, in the story, Naomi learns of Boaz through Ruth. (The implications of that subtlety is left to the diligent.)

The exposition of the almost inexhaustible "coding" aspects of this tiny book exceeds the space available here.[197]

It is also interesting that this pivotal book is also associated with the Feast of *Shavout*, the Feast of Pentecost. Coincidence? Hardly.

Chapters 6 through 18 of the Book of Revelation detail the strange and climactic events which precede the establishment of Christ's kingdom upon the Earth. These are simply an expansion of the final seven-year period also known as the 70th Week of the prophecy Gabriel delivered to Daniel.[198]

Joshua as a Macrocode

The Book of Joshua in the Old Testament also appears to be an anticipatory structural model of the Book of Revelation. The very name is *Yehoshua*, is a variant of the Hebrew name *Yeshua* which has been Anglecized from the Greek to get

"Jesus." Joshua was the military leader leading God's people to possess the land that God had given them, dispossessing the usurpers. The Book of Revelation casts Jesus Christ in the identical role: dispossessing the usurpers from the Planet Earth.

When God told Abraham that his descendants would inherit the land,[199] Satan had 400 years to lay down a minefield. The Rephaim and other tribes ("giants") planted in Canaan were post-flood *Nephilim* that again were his attempt to thwart the Plan of God.[200] Joshua was the military warrior who led a seven-year campaign to deal with the seven (of an original ten) nations.

The Amorites were the largest of the seven tribes, and the first battle was against the capital of the Amorites, Jericho.[201] But who really was the leader at the battle of Jericho? With all due deference to the famed song, it wasn't Joshua that "fought the battle of Jericho." Joshua yielded to a warrior-leader that was the "Captain of the Lord's Host."[202] This was not an ordinary angel: angels do not allow themselves to be worshiped; this one not only commands worship, he used the very words that Joshua would recognize from his previous encounter at Mount Sinai 40 years earlier.[203] It was an Old Testament appearance of Jesus.[204]

Before the attack on Jericho, Joshua sends in two "spies." Why? Some assume that two were sent because forty years earlier, when Moses sent in twelve, only two were fruitful! Ten were intimidated by the *Nephilim* in the land; and the timidity of the people resulted in being condemned to the wilderness wanderings for forty years.[205]

But just what did the two "spies" accomplish? They certainly didn't bring back military intelligence that resulted in the peculiar battle plan. Can you imagine Joshua's meeting with his general staff, presenting his strategy to take the city? "We are going to march around the city once a day for six days, keeping silence. Then on the seventh day, we are going to march around seven times and then blow our horns and then the walls will fall down." Sure. No problem.

The only thing the two "spies" accomplished was to get Rahab saved. Could they be analogous to the two "witnesses" that precede the tribulations of Revelation Chapter 11?

The battle of Jericho itself is a collection of mysteries. It seems to have violated every ordinance of the Torah: the Levites were exempt from military duties, yet they led the procession.[206] They were supposed to work for six days but rest on the seventh; yet at Jericho they marched seven times as much on the seventh day.

This seems to follow the pattern anticipating the seven trumpet judgments in Revelation 8 and 9. It is interesting that Joshua instructed them to *maintain silence* until the final series of seven on the seventh day;[207] in Revelation we have a strange period of silence prior to the seven trumpets.[208]

Joshua ultimately encounters an alliance of nations under a leader who calls himself, *Adoni-Zedek* ("Lord of Righteousness"), who is finally defeated in the battle of Beth-Horon with signs in the sun and moon,[209] in which the kings hide themselves in caves, etc.[210] The parallels in Revelation are striking.

Implications For Today

What does the Gaza Strip and the Golan Heights have in common with *today?* It is interesting that these were the places that Joshua failed to totally exterminate the Rephaim and Anakim (*Nephilim*); these were the strongholds of Israel's enemies then, and they remain so today!

We believe that we are being plunged into a period of time about which the Bible says more than it does about any other period of time in history, *including the time that Jesus walked the shores of Galilee and climbed the mountains of Judea!*

That's a preposterous statement. If you accept that view, you flunk the course: I hope you *challenge* it! How do you do that? You must accomplish two things:

1) Find out what the Bible says about the future. About Israel; about Jerusalem; about the rebuilding of the Temple. Find out about the major themes of prophecy: the rise of a European Superstate; the rise of China as a super power; about the rebuilding of Babylon; about the impending invasion by Russia of the Middle East.

2) Find out what is really going on. That's the hard part. You won't find out on the Ten O'Clock News. The media has its own agenda: to *form* public opinion rather than *inform* it. With the alternative press, talk radio, and the Internet, it's easier to find out the truth, *if you're committed to it.*

But we are, indeed, in interesting times. And the Bible is the only reliable guide to the real truth. We hope this brief review was stimulating, provocative, and, perhaps, disturbing.

Selection Fourteen

Where Next?

The primary significance of these little "hidden treasures" is not to convey any "new" doctrinal information, but rather to *authenticate* the supernatural origin of the whole, and to elevate our understanding of, and respect for, the integrity of the Scriptures. Everything else will derive from both our comprehension and our confidence in the Word of God. We hope these nuggets, from years of collecting, has proven helpful.

Most of these brief examples have been excerpted from our definitive study, *Cosmic Codes - Hidden Messages From the Edge of Eternity*. If you are interested in exploring in more depth the many different types of codes and ciphers in the Bible, we encourage you to explore it. (It has been recognized as the definitive study of the many types of "Bible Codes," Equidistant Letter Sequences being but one of them.)

It is our hope that you have found some of these provocative and that they have stimulated a desire to study further. For a strategic grasp of the entire Bible–and a more comprehensive view of the integrity of its design–we encourage you to undertake *Learn the Bible in 24 Hours*, an intensive series of one-hour presentations, with computer assisted diagrams, that is available on a CD-ROM. (The audio presentations are also available on tape cassettes.) This is a quick way to get a broad foundation, and it is also a refreshing offset to our tendency to focus on just our favorite passages or specialties.

Our hope is that this, in turn, will lead you to want to study each specific book of the Bible in more detail, so we also offer verse-by-verse *Expositional Commentaries,* on either audio tape cassettes or on CD-ROMs, and both include extensive notes and references. (The CD-ROMs feature audio in MP3 format, permitting downloading to the popular pocket players, and the notes and diagrams in PDF format. The necessary software is included for both.)

The facility of audio recordings have proven to be a quick way to get up to speed on any subject; and when accompanied by appropriate notes (or computer assisted diagrams), the personal progress one can make, at his/her own convenience, is unparalleled.

We also publish a monthly news journal which highlights the Biblical relevance of current events, including geopolitical developments, scientific and archaeological discoveries, as well as provocative background articles intended to encourage your taking the Bible seriously as the inerrant Word of God. A gift certificate for a year's subscription has been included in the back of this book. Or just call us at (800) KHOUSE1.

Also, check out our Internet website at www.khouse.org. You can also sign up for our weekly *eNews* bulletins; they're free.

Meanwhile, we hope this book has stimulated you to learn more about the Bible, and discover more about the person it is all about: our Lord Jesus Christ. *He* is what it is really all about.

End Notes:

1.   Job was far earlier than even the books of Moses.

2   There are examples in particle physics where a positron is understood to be an electron in a time reversal. See *Beyond Time and Space,* and *Beyond Perception,* audio briefings with notes, Koinonia House.

3   The ancient Hebrew scholar Nachmonides, writing in the 12th century, concluded from his studies of Genesis that the universe had 10 dimensions—only four are knowable, with six are beyond our knowing. It is interesting that particle physicists today have concluded that we live in 10 dimensions: 3 spatial dimensions and time are directly measureable. The remaining 6 are "curled" in less than 10^{-33} cm. and are only inferable by indirect means. (See *Beyond Perception,* Koinonia House.)

4.   Lorentz transformation: $Ts = Te / (1 - v^2/c^2)^{\frac{1}{2}}$.

5   Isaiah 57:15.

6   Isaiah 46:10.

7   Examples: *The Sovereignty of Man, The Architecture of Man,* or *From Here to Eternity—the Physics of Immortality* , all available from Koinonia House.

8.   Published in *Personal UPDATE,* most recently 2/96, p.19-23.

9.   Genesis 5:24.

10.   "*Muth,*" death, occurs 125 times in the Old Testament.

11.   See Pink, Jones, and Stedman in Bibliography.

12.   Gen 5:25-28.

13.   Gen 7:6,11.

14.   Genesis 5:27.

15.   Genesis 4:25.

16.   Gen 4:26 is often mistranslated. *Targum of Onkelos:* "...desisted from praying in the name"; *Targum of Jonathan:* "surnamed their idols in the name..."; Kimchi, Rashi, and other ancient Jewish commentators agree. Jerome indicated that this was the opinion of many Jews of his day. Maimonides, *Commentary on the Mishna* (a constituent part of the *Talmud*), A.D. 1168, ascribes the origin of idolatry to the days of Enosh.

17.   Numbers 24:21,23.

18.   These were discussed in our book, *Alien Encounters,* from this publisher.

19.   Gen 5:21,24.

20.   Gen 4:19-25; rabbinical sources, Re: Kaplan, et al.

21.   Isaiah 46:10; Revelation 21:6; 22:13.

22   Bachya was not the first to notice encrypted information in the Torah.

23   Satinover, pp.56-65.

24   Dr. Gerald L. Schroeder, *Genesis and the Big Bang,* Bantam Books, New York, 1990.

25   In Deuteronomy, it starts from the 5th verse, and the interval is 49. These variations are dealt with by Professor Daniel Michelson in his famous article, "Codes in the Torah" in *B'Or Ha'Torah*, No. 6, 1987.

26.   In Psalm 46, if you count 46 words from the beginning, you find "shake." If you count 46 words back from the end, you find "spear." The legend is that William Shakespear, during the 1611 translation of what became the King James Version, hid this bid for immortality when celebrating his 46th birthday. Colorful, but not taken too seriously by scholars.

27.   See our book, *Cosmic Codes - Hidden Messages From the Edge of Eternity*, for comprehensive review. This book has been recognized as the definitive source and was used in the recent prime time TV specials.

28.   McCormack, R., *The Heptadic Structure of Scripture*, Marshall Brothers Ltd., London, 1923; E.W. Bullinger, *Numbers of the Scriptures*, Kregel Publications, Grand Rapids MI, reproduction from 1894; F. W. Grant, *The Numerical Bible*, (7 vols.); Browne, *Ordo Saeculoreium*, et al.

29.   Ivan Panin was born in Russia on December 12, 1855. Having participated in plots against the Czar at an early age, he was exiled and after spending some years in study in Germany, came to the United States and entered Harvard University. After graduation in 1882, he converted from agnosticism to Christianity. In 1890 he discovered some of the phenomenal mathematical design underlying both the Greek text of the New Testament and the Hebrew text of the Old Testament. He was to devote over 50 years of his life painstakingly–and exhausting his health–exploring the numerical structure of the Scriptures, generating over 43,000 detailed hand-penned pages of analysis. He went on to be with the Lord in his 87th year, on October 30, 1942.

30.   These are detailed in our briefing package, *How We Got Our Bible*, from this same publisher.

31.   Hebrew *ammah* ("mother of the arm"), the fore-arm, was the nominal distance from one's elbow to the fingertip; the term "cubit" is from the Latin *cubitus*, the lower arm.

32.   The answer to this difficulty was discovered by Shlomo Edward G. Belaga that appeared in Boaz Tsaban's Rabbinical Math page on the Internet, <www.cs.biu.ac.il:8080/~tsaban/hebrew.html> .

33.   There were several "official" cubits in the ancient world, varying from about 18 inches to almost two feet. Some authorities assume 20.24 inches for the ordinary cubit , and 21.888 inches for the sacred one. We have used 18 inches in the discussion.

34.   Driver, *Notes on the Hebrew Text and the Topography of the Books of Samuel*, The Clarendon Press, Oxford, 1913, p.97; R..A. H. Gunner, "Number," *The New Bible Dictionary*, Wm. B. Eerdmans Publishing Co., Grand Rapids MI 1963, p.895.

35. W. F. Albright, "The Lachish Letters After Five Years," *Bulletin of the American Schools of Oriental Researh,* No. 22, April 1941.

36. Merrill Unger, *Unger's Bible Dictionary*, Moody Press, Chicago, 1957, p.799.

37. Genesis 49:10.

38. Ruth 4:22; 2 Samuel 7:11-16.

39. Matthew 1:1-17.

40. Luke 3:23-38. According to Lachmann, Tischendorf, Tregelles, Alford, Westcott and Hort: νομίζω, *nomizo,* reckoned as by law. Joseph was the son-in-law of Heli, having married his only daughter Mary. (*Jerusalem Talmud, Chag.*77,4.) Cf. E. W. Bullinger, *Number in Scripture*, Kregel, Grand Rapids MI, from 1894 reproduction, p.160 note.

41. Numbers 26:33; 27:1-11; 36:2-12; Joshua 17:3-6; 1 Chronicles 7:15.

42. Cf. Ezra 2:61 & Neh 7:63; Num 32:41; 1 Chron 2:21-23, 34-35. Luke 3:23, νομίζω *nomizo*, reckoned as by law.

43 Matthew 24 & 25; Mark 13 & 14, and Luke 21 & 22.

44 Matthew 24:15.

45 Daniel 9:2; Jeremiah 25:11, 12.

46 For a more complete discussion, see our briefing package, *The Seventy Weeks of Daniel*, two audio cassettes plus extensive notes. Also, *Expositional Commentary on Daniel*, 3 volumes, available from Koinonia House.

47. The seven months between Nisan and Tishri contain the seven feasts between Passover through Succot.

48 Genesis 29:26-28; Leviticus 25, 26. A sabbath for the land ordained for every week of years: Leviticus 25:1-22; 26:33-35; Deuteronomy 15; Exodus 23:10, 11. Failure to keep the sabbath of the land was basis for their 70 years captivity: 2 Chronicles 36:19-21.

49 A fascinating conjecture as to the cause of this calendar change is detailed in *Signs in the Heavens,* a briefing package exploring the "long day" of Joshua and the possible orbital antics of the Planet Mars.

50 The 3rd, 6th, 8th, 11th, 14th, 17th and 19th are leap years, where the month *Adar II* is added. Originally kept secret by the Sanhedrin, the method of calendar intercalation was revealed in the 4th century, when an independent Sanhedrin was threatened, to permit the diaspora Jews to observe in synchronization. Arthur Spier, *The Comprehensive Hebrew Calendar*, Feldheim Publishers, Jerusalem, 1986.

51 Genesis 7:24; 8:3,4, etc. In Revelation, 42 months = 3 1/2 years = 1260 days, etc. We are indebted to Sir Robert Anderson's classic, *The Coming Prince*, originally published in 1894, for this insight.

52 Nehemiah 2:5-8, 17, 18. There were three other decrees, but they were concerned with the rebuilding of the Temple, not the cityand the walls: Cyrus, 537 B.C., Ezra 1:2-4; Darius, Ezra 6:1-5, 8, 12; Artaxerxes, 458 B.C. Ezra

7:11-26.

53   The English Bible translates *Nagid* as "prince." However, it should be "king." *Nagid* is first used of King Saul.

54   John 6:15; 7:30, 44; etc.

55   Luke 19:29-48. Cf. Matt 21, Mark 11.

56   Recorded in all 4 Gospels: Matthew 21:1-9; Mark 11:1-10; Luke 19:29-39; John 12:12-16.

57   The Hallel Psalm 118: note verse 26.

58   This was the day that passover lambs were being presented for acceptability. Four days later, Jesus would be offered as our Passover.

59   Luke 3:1: Tiberius appointed, 14 A.D.; + 15th year = 29 A.D.. 4th Passover, 32 A.D. (April 6).

60.   See Risto Santala, *The Messiah in the Old Testament in the Light of Rabbinical Writings*, and *The Messiah in the New Testament in the Light of Rabbinical Writings*, [translated from the Finnish; first published in Hebrew] Keren Ahvah Meshihi, Jerusalem, 1992; and Mark Eastman, *The Search for the Messiah*, The Word For Today, Costa Mesa CA 1993.

61.   ἁρπαγησόμεθα, is a verb, indicative future passive 1st person plural, from ἁρπάζω (aorist. passive), to take by force; take away, carry off; catch up.

62.   Hosea 5:15. See our briefing package, *The Next Holocaust and the Refuge in Edom* for a summary of this view. Also, Arnold Fruchtenbaum, *Footsteps of the Messiah*, Ariel Press, Tustin CA 1982.

63.   Flavius Josephus, *Wars of the Jews*, Book VI, Chapter 1.

64   Leviticus 7:20; Psalm 37:9; Proverbs 2:22; Isaiah 53:7-9.

65   Interval also implied: Daniel 9:26; Isaiah 61:1, 2 (Re: Luke 4:18-20); Revelation 12:5, 6. Also: Isaiah 54:7; Hosea 3:4, 5; Amos 9:10, 11; (Acts 15:13-18); Micah 5:2, 3; Zechariah 9:9, 10; Luke 1:31,3 2; 21:24. There are actually 24 allusions to this interval, which may be linked to the 24 elders in Revelation. See *Cosmic Codes,* Chapter 18.

66   Luke 19:42 until Romans 11:25.

67   Matthew 13:34, 35; Ephesians 3:5, 9.

68.   Sir Robert Anderson, *The Coming Prince*, 1894.

69.   Matthew 13:10-16.

70.   We use the term "prototype" for an anticipatory model in engineering, etc.

71.   Genesis 14:18-20.

72.   1 Chronicles 24:15-28; 2 Chronicles 3:1.

73.   Isaiah 53; Psalm 22; et al.

74.   Genesis 22:2.

75. John 3:16.

76. Genesis 3:21.

77. Genesis 17:19; 21:12. Also, Hebrews 11:17-19.

78. It is interesting that in the numerous "Gentile bride" types in the Scripture, none of them have their death recorded. Is this part of a macrocode design?

79. Genesis 15:2. It is instructive to notice that whenever the Holy Spirit emerges as a type, it is as an unnamed servant. Ruth, later to become the bride of Boaz, the Kinsman-Redeemer, is first introduced to him by his unnamed servant: Ruth 2:5, 6. Jesus explained why in John 16:13.

80. Genesis 24:62.

81. Ex. 25-27; 36-38; 40.

82. For an in-depth study of the Tabernacle, review *The Mystery of the Lost Ark* Briefing Package.

83. Gen 41:37-41.

84. Gen 48.

85. Gen 29, 35; 46; 49, Ex 1; Num 1:1-15; 1:20-43; 2:7; 10; 13; 26; 34; Deut 27; 33; Josh 13ff; Jud 5; 1 Chron 2:1; 2:3-8; 12; 27; Eze 48; Rev 7.

86. Job 38:32.

87. Genesis 11:1-9.

88. For an in depth study of the 12 tribes, refer to our *Expositional Commentary on Joshua*, volume 2.

89. John 12:23, 24, 27.

90. Gen 3:15. See also Gen 15:5 and Gal 3:16 (seed is singular not plural).

91. Isa 4:2: "The Branch of the Lord," a title for Jesus Christ; Jer 23:5 and 33:15: a royal King from line of David; Zech 3:8: servant of Jehovah; Zech 6:12: will build the Temple.

92. Isaiah 4:2.

93. Psalm 72:8.

94. For further study review our briefing package, *Signs in the Heavens*, or the other references in the bibliography.

95. Eze 1:10; 10:14; Rev 4:7. (Some feel that the *seraphim* in Isaish 6 are the same.)

96. Numbers 2.

97. Ezekiel 1:10; 10:14; Revelation 4:7.

98. Num 2:3, 10, 18, 25.

99. Haggai 2:7.

100.   Isaiah 53:3.

101.   Jeremiah 33:10.

102.   Zechariah 12:10.

103.   Exodus 3:13, 14; Rev 1:8.

104.   Psalm 96:13; Revelation 14:14-16.

105.   Job 9:9.

106.   Zechariah 12:10.

107.   Luke 4:16-21. Cf. Isaiah 61:1-2.

108.   Randall Price, *Secrets of the Dead Sea Scrolls,* Harvest House Publishers, Eugene OR 1996, p.126.

109.   E. Y. Kuscher, *The Language and Linguistic Background of the Isaiah Scroll (1QIsa^a),* E.J. Brill, Leiden 1974, and Elisha Qimron, *Indices and Corrections,* 1979.

110.   Yacov Rambsel, *Yeshua - The Hebrew Factor,* and *His Name is Jesus*; and Grant Jeffrey's *The Signature of God,* and *The Handwriting of God,* all published by Frontier Research Publications, Toronto Ontario Canada, 1996 and 1997, respectively.

111.   The common appellation of a "carpenter" may be a mistranslation. The term τέκτων actually means builder.

112.   Isaiah 53:4 and 5, each with an interval of -32 (in reverse). The term is encoded 70 times in the Book of Isaiah.

113.   Luke 3:2.

114.   John W. Lawrence, *The Six Trials of Jesus*, Kregel Publications, Grand Rapids MI 1977.

115.   Grant Jeffrey reports it as occurring in Isaiah 53:5, starting with the 3rd letter in the tenth word, at intervals of -133 (in reverse). We couldn't find it there, but it appeared in Isaiah 53:3 at a reverse interval of -82; and also in Isaiah 53:6 and a forward interval of 85.

116.   This name appears, using intervals up to 100, 1149 times in the Old Testament, forward 774 times (including 350 without any interval), and in reverse 375 times. In Isaiah, it appears 101 times (forward 73 times, in reverse, 28 times).

117.   Matt. 4:21; 10:2; Mark 1:19; 3:17.

118.   Matt. 17:1; Mark 3:17; 5:37; Acts 12:2.

119.   Matt. 4:21; Mark 1:19-20; Luke 5:10-11.

120.   Mark 3:17.

121.   Matt. 10:2-4; Mark 3:16-19; Luke 6:14-16; Acts 1:13.

122.   Mark 5:37; Luke 8:51.

123. Matt. 17:1; Mark 9:2; Luke 9:28.

124. Mark 13:3.

125. Matt. 26:37; Mark 14:33.

126. Acts 12:2.

127. Mt. 10:3; Acts 1:13.

128. Mark 15:40.

129. Mt. 13:55.

130. Compare Mark. 3:21 and John 7:5.

131. 1 Cor. 15:7.

132. Gal. 1:19; 2:9; Acts 12:17. Recent archeological discoveries have confirmed James' role as leader in Jerusalem.

133. Josephus, *Antiquities,* 20. 9.

134. Jeffrey, *Handwriting,* p.155.

135. Grant Jeffrey reports a comparable list of codes in Exodus 30:16, a passage which deals with God's commands regarding the atonement for sins. See Grant Jeffrey, *The Handwriting of God*, Frontier Research Publications, Toronto Ontario, 1997, pp.172-173.

136. The prophetic role of the feast days are in Chapter 10.

137. Mount Moriah is the ridge that has Golgatha at its peak. See page 57.

138. Mark 15:40.

139. It is interesting that the elements of bread and wine have the same interval.

140. Acts 1:23-26.

141. Wetzel Publishing Company, Los Angeles CA, 1939.

142. Genesis 11:1.

143. For a more detailed review, see the book, *Alien Encounters*, by Drs. Mark Eastman and Chuck Missler, Koinonia House, 1996.

144. Lev 23; Num 28-29; Deut 16.

145. Lev 23:4.

146. Romans 15:4; Galatians 3:24, 25.

147. Colossians 2:16, 17.

148. Ex 12:1-14, 43-48; Lev 23:5.

149. Exodus 4:23. ("Firstborn" being a term of favored position and inheritance, not necessarily of direct issue.)

150. Gen 15:13-16; Galatians 3:16, 17.

151. Contrary to the impression suggested by Cecil B. DeMille's famous movie, *The Ten Commandments*, this was predicted by God when He first called Moses: Exodus 4:23.

152. Observed by Immanuel Velikovski in his noteworthy book, *Worlds in Collision,* published in 1950.

153. Ex 12:1-13; Lev 23:4, 5,

154. Ex 12:46; Num 9:12; Psa 34:20.

155. John 1:29, 36.

156. 1 Corinthians 5:7.

157. 1 Pet 1:18-20.

158. John 19:4.

159. John 19:31-33, 36.

160. Lev 17:11; Matt 26:27, 28.

161. 1 Corinthians 10:16.

162. *Mishna*, Pes. VII 13.

163. Lev 23:6-8.

164. Deut 16:16.

165. This is generally attributed to its origin in the heart of Lucifer: Isaiah 14:12-14.

166. Ex 12:15; 13:7; Lev 2:11; 6:17;10:12.

167. Matt 16:6; Luke 13:21; 1 Cor 5:6-8; Gal 5:7-9.

168. The parable of The Woman and The Leaven (Matt 13:33) is often misunderstood due to a lack of understanding of this background.

169. Isaiah 53:5 (q.v. 1 Peter 2:24); Psalm 22:16; Zechariah 12:10; John 19:34, 37; Revelation 1:7.

170. John 6:31-35; 47-51.

171. Exodus 16:15, 31-35; Numbers 11:6-9; Deuteronomy 8:2, 16.

172. Genesis 14:18.

173. Genesis 40:1-23.

174. Leviticus 23:11.

175. 1 Cor 15:20-23; Matt 27:52-53; Rom 11:16 (cf. Job 19:25-26).

176. Exodus 12:2.

177. Matthew 12:40. This opens the issue of the day of the week that Jesus was crucified: was it really on a Friday? Or Wenesday or Thursday? There are good scholars on both sides of this controversy. However, there are some substantial

Scriptural evidences that it could not (despite the church traditions) have been on a Friday: Jesus, as an observant Jew, could not have indulged in the trip from Ephraim to Bethany on a Sabbath day the week before: John 11:54; 12:1.

178. These last two references may be upsetting to Jehovah's Witnesses who have their own unique views on these identities.

179. There are numerous allusions in the Old Testament of the execution of the Messiah of Israel: Psalm 22; Isaiah 52:12-53:12; Daniel 9:24-27; Zechariah 12:10.

180. This was excerpted from *Personal UPDATE* of September 1993, pp.12-13.

181. E.W. Bullinger, *Figures of Speech Used in the Bible,* Eyre and Spottiswoode, London, 1898, p. 833.

182. For a comprehensive catalog of over 200 rhetorical devices used in the Bible, see *Cosmic Codes*, Appendix A.

183. Bullinger, *Figures*, p.744.

184. Cf. Colossians 1:16ff.

185. Joshua 11:23; 18:10.

186. Numbers 18:20.

187. Number 35:2-7; Joshua 21:41.

188. Numbers 35:15-34.

189. Acts 2:23.

190. Luke 23:34.

191. Hebrews 2:17; 3:1; 4:14-15; 5:1, 5, 10; 8:1; 9:11, et al.

192. Romans 8:1.

193. Isaiah 46:10; Acts 15:18. Cf. Isaiah 41:22,23 44:7 45:21 Genesis 3:15 12:2,3 49:10,22 26 Numbers 24:17-24; Deuteronomy 4:24-31 28:15.

194. A fee simple estate of inheritance is one which devolves to the owner's heirs and assigns forever without limitation.

195. An example of this was when Jeremiah, despite the impending Babylonian captivity, was instructed to purchase land from the son of his uncle Hanameel. He, of course, would never benefit from this purchase. The deed was secreted in an earthen jar in anticipation when his heirs would return after the captivity and claim it. Jeremiah 32:6-15.

196. In addition to the Law of Redemption (Leviticus 25:47-50), one must understand the Law of Leverite Marriage (Deuteronomy 25:5-10).

197. See *The Romance of Redemption - Gleanings from the Book of Ruth*, from this publisher.

198. Daniel 9:24-27.

199. Genesis 15:13-21.

200. See *Alien Encounters* from this publisher.

201. Jericho is named after the Moon God. It is interesting that it is the base for the PLO today.

202. Joshua 5:13-15.

203. Exodus 3:5; Joshua 5:15. Cf. Rev 19:10; 22:9. One angel did seek worship and caused a lot of trouble: Lucifer, now known as Satan. (Isaiah 14:12-17; Ezekiel 28:12-19.)

204. Josh 5:13-15. Cf. Zech 14:3; Number 21:14.

205. Numbers 13 & 14.

206. Number 1:45, 49; 31; Joshua 6:4f.

207. Joshua 6:10.

208. Revelation 8:1.

209. Joshua 10:12, 13. Cf. Rev 6:12; 8:12.

210. Joshua 10:16-24. Cf. Rev 6:15, 16.

What is
Koinonia House ?

Koinonia House is a publishing ministry dedicated to creating, developing and distributing materials to stimulate, encourage and facilitate serious study of the Bible as the inerrant Word of God.

A certificate for an initial year's subscription to our monthly *Personal UPDATE* News Journal has been included at the end of this book.

For more information please write

Koinonia House
P.O. Box D
Coeur d'Alene, Idaho
83816-0347

Or call:
1-800-KHOUSE-1

Visit us on the Internet at:
www.khouse.org

Koinonia House Canada
P.O. Box 392
Cranbrook, B.C. Canada
V1C 4H9
Phone (250)417-0837
canada@khouse.org

Koinonia House Europe
P.O. Box 188
Portsmouth
PO8 9GP England
Phone +44 (0) 23 9257 0338
europe@khouse.org

Koinonia House Australia
P.O. Box 2110
Tuggeranong ACT 2901
Phone +61.2-6273-3652
australia@khouse.org

Koinonia House New Zealand
12 Seine Road, Milford,
Auckland
Phone +64 9 410 1929
nz@khouse.org

How Did We Get Our Bible?

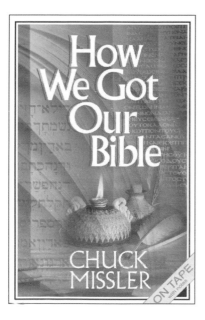

Where did our Bible come from?

Why do we believe its origin is supernatural?

How do we know that it really is the Word of God?

How accurate are our translations? Which version of the Bible is the best? Chuck Missler, an internationally recognized authority, reviews the origin of both the Old Testament and the New Testament in light of recent discoveries and controversies. This study is foundational for every Christian.

All briefing packages contain two audio cassettes and extensive study notes.

Visit us on the Internet at:
www.khouse.org

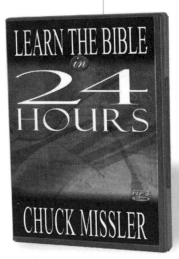

About the Author

Chuck Missler

Dr. Chuck Missler is an Honor Graduate of the United States Naval Academy, Annapolis, Maryland; he has a Master's Degree in Engineering from the University of California at Los Angeles, and a PhD from Louisiana Baptist University, with supplemental graduate studies in Applied Mathematics, Advanced Statistics, and the Information Sciences.

In his 30-year executive career, Dr. Missler has served on over a dozen Boards of Directors of public companies and has served as Chairman and Chief Executive Officer of six of them.

Dr. Missler has taught Bible studies for over 30 years, has been featured on numerous national television shows, and his daily radio broadcasts are heard in a dozen countries worldwide.

Dr. Missler has authored over 100 publications, including *Expositional Commentaries* on 40 books of the Bible, and was an invited contributor to the *Dictionary of Premillennial Theology* (Mal Couch, Gen. Ed., Kregel Publications, Grand Rapids MI 1996); the *Prophecy Study Bible* (Tim LaHaye, Ed., AMG Publishers, 2000); and is on the review committee of *The International Standard Version*, a new translation of the Bible.

$20.00 Value

$20.00 Value

Certificate

This certificate entitles the person below to a full year's subscription to *Personal* **UPDATE**, a newsletter highlighting the Biblical relevance of current events. (New subscribers only.)

Name: _____

Address: _____

City: _____ State: _____ Zip: _____

Koinonia House, P.O. Box D, Coeur d'Alene ID 83816-0347

HT1